FOUR ES

Facing Spelling as Student and Teacher

Melvin J. Hoffman

University Press of America,® Inc.
Dallas · Lanham · Boulder · New York · Oxford

Copyright © 2004 by
University Press of America,® Inc.
4501 Forbes Boulevard
Suite 200
Lanham, Maryland 20706
UPA Acquisitions Department (301) 459-3366

PO Box 317
Oxford
OX2 9RU, UK

British Library Cataloging in Publication Information Available

Library of Congress Control Number: 2003111863
ISBN 0-7618-2735-8 (paperback : alk. ppr.)

⊖™ The paper used in this publication meets the minimum
requirements of American National Standard for Information
Sciences—Permanence of Paper for Printed Library Materials,
ANSI Z39.48—1984

To Katherine M. Hoffman for being what a mother is expected to be and to Maureen M. Moll for not being what a mother-in-law is expected to be

CONTENTS

ACKNOWLEDGEMENTS

My spouse Jennifer M. Hoffman, a professional librarian, has influenced my trying to broaden the audience for this book. She has made me aware that there is an audience for factual as well as fictional works, provided that they are reasonably comprehensible and minimally technical.

Dr. Geraldine E. Bard is an English Department colleague and fellow linguist. With unflagging zeal, she promotes the application of linguistic concepts and information to ameliorate pedagogical and social problems. She is not only an advocate, but also a model for such applied linguistic research. She is one of the guiding lights behind Project F.L.I.G.H.T. (Family Literacy for Intergenerational Teaching) which has received local, national and international recognition

Dr. Susan M. Leist is an English Department colleague and a specialist in writing across the curriculum and in preparation of elementary and secondary education teachers. While team teaching a course together, I presented a unit on spelling using some of the material in this book. Dr. Leist was adamant in the conviction that the information was worthy of an audience beyond the classroom.

Also, I must note colleagues who share information, and provide a collegially nurturing environment for publication. They are Drs. Ann C. Colley, Marvin J. LaHood, David E. Lampe and Zan D. Robinson. I apologize to others whom I may have inadvertently missed.

The format, categories and presentation of multiple spelling systems in this book are my own. However, the principle of multiple English spelling systems is based upon work of two linguists, the late Dr. Henry Lee Smith Jr. and Emeritus Professor Henry J. Sustakoski. Dr. Henry Lee Smith Jr. was my advisor and thesis director at the State University of New York at Buffalo. I started work with him in Anthropology and finished in the Linguistic Department which had separated subsequently from the former.

Professor Henry J. Sustakoski and I were graduate students together at the University. Later, I became his colleague in the Department of English at Buffalo State University College. Just before my arrival, he and Dr. Smith had finished their joint work which I cite in my bibliography.

Finally, I wish to acknowledge the chair of my Department, and the former and present of Deans of Arts and Humanities. They are, respectively, Drs. Kevin J. Railey, Steven A. Kaplan, and Emile C. Netzhammer III. They are the people largely responsible for schedule changes in the English Department. Such changes enabled me to set aside blocks of time to polish and finish this book which I had started much earlier.

Buffalo State University College 2003

Chapter 1

SPELLING, ME AND ORTHOGRAPY

My intention is to make this work on spelling accessible to as large an audience as may be interested in new approaches. Therefore, it lacks clinical reports of research results, exhaustive sets of statistics and series of supporting graphs.

Replacing theoretical elaborations are selective examples illustrating what is being discussed. Further, there is a limit in technical terminology to the minimally necessary. This does not mean that its contents have bases neither in theory nor in research. Instead, sources blend considerations from both linguistic and etymological research with commentary from both personal observations and experiences.

The information and explanations draw from personal as well as from professional, engagement with spelling. Some circumstances, I share with other native speakers and writers of English. Other particulars are less typical, involving graduate training as a linguist and classroom experiences as a teacher of writing.

For some people, spelling is far from a cut-and-dried learning activity which is eventually mastered. Rather, spelling is something to contend with in some form, and at various times, throughout life.

This presenter who has grappled with spelling both as pupil and professor introduces an alternative way to address English spelling mastery problems. Some spelling problems are more subtle than those commonly identified and treated.

The alternative depends upon particular linguistic points of view. After some explanations and examples, the new perspectives lead to a rethinking of applications for spelling improvement.

OUT OF DIAPERS AND INTO PRIMERS

Like most other English speakers, spelling constituted an important part of my early education. Formal grading on spelling continued through secondary English courses up until first-year composition courses.

Thereafter, instructors in various courses, not only English, occasionally graded spelling, among other things, in reports, term papers, projects etc. I spelled well enough to satisfy the requirements of these venues.

My spelling was no better, initially, than most classmates. Like most of those fellow students, wrestling with a number of common problems was my lot.

Fortunately, by means available, most spelling deficiencies were overcome before high school graduation. Some teacher and textbook approaches which were helpful, here systematically reanalyzed and illustrated, form one among several strands woven into this presentation.

Later, graduate training as a linguist presented an opportunity to learn about various writing systems representing both ancient and modern languages. Particular emphasis was placed upon syllabic and alphabetic systems which had letter and sound correspondences.

Among other goals for linguistics' students was to learn to evaluate sound to symbol correspondences. This was to determine how well sound systems were mapped by written representations of them.

Training helped budding linguists to understand the relationship of writing to speech far better than before. Such students could design an excellent alphabet for an unwritten language, at least theoretically. They also learned that sound and character, or meaning and character, were not the sole considerations in adopting or designing writing systems.

An online bibliography "Social Aspects of Orthography" (Sebba 1995) includes a number of sources dealing with varied societal contexts. Among such issues addressed are the creation and/or introduction of a writing system, spelling reform and effects of writing upon language. Part III of Trager (1972) treats related concerns.

The very existence of writing affects the language itself as well as the language habits of its speakers. This is true regardless of whether the writing system is original or borrowed.

The English alphabet borrowed from the Romans. The Romans borrowed from the Greeks who borrowed from Semitic alphabets.

OTHER FOLKS AND THEIR ALPHABETS

There are many occurrences in history of one society borrowing a preexisting writing system from another. Writing systems may be borrowed for varied reasons.

People may adopt the language of a prestige group or conqueror for considerations of politics, economics, survival etc. A society or group may also borrow liturgical languages of societies from which the group has adopted a religion.

A people may wish to write their own unwritten language to preserve history, customs, laws etc. which otherwise might be lost. Again, some people with unwritten languages might wish for their language to achieve the status which they perceive written languages to have.

The origins and types of writing systems vary greatly. The following inventory represents just a very small sample of the variety that exists. They do show that writing itself is a far more complex matter than just the representation of sounds or meanings by symbols.

Korean has an indigenous writing system. Inuit has borrowed three writing systems: a Roman alphabet, a Cyrillic alphabet and a syllabary, all devised by missionaries. Cherokee uses western alphabetic characters but with non-European pronunciations; in fact, the characters represent syllables instead of individual sounds.

Some languages have more than one writing system due to changing historical circumstances such as political, social or religious divisions among their speakers.

The language, Aramaic, (which in later Christian forms is called Syriac) has four writing systems. The Aramaic is very similar to the modern Hebrew writing system. The earliest Syriac script is called "Estrangelo."

Two latter scripts descended from this. The Eastern descendant is called "Nestorian;" the Western is termed "Serto."

Languages of the same southern Slavic origin, Serbian and Croatian, share great similarities in sound system and grammar. However, they have differentiated their vocabulary over time.

Serbian, with mostly Eastern Orthodox speakers, was externally influenced by Greek and Russian. Croatian, with mostly Roman Catholic speakers, was externally influenced by Latin, German and other western European languages.

During the existence of Tito's Yugoslavia, political pressure existed to reunify the two languages. The official name for this somewhat artificially recreated entity was Serbo-Croatian.

Serbo-Croatian had two alphabets which were adapted from the Roman and Cyrillic alphabet respectively. Croatian also had had an earlier alphabet: Glagolitic.

Hindustani is a language spoken now, as well as earlier, in both India and Pakistan. It is also the ancestor of two related literary languages: Hindi and Urdu.

Hindi, spoken mostly by Hindus, uses a Sanskrit based syllabary, "Devanagiri," and has preserved or reborrowed many Sanskrit words. Urdu, spoken mostly by Muslims, has an Arabic derived alphabet with many word borrowings from Persian, Arabic and Turkish.

ENGLISH AND ITS WRITING SYSTEMS

Many societies adopt the writing systems of admired neighbors. In the latter case, borrowers may want to preserve every donor language letter or character whether necessary in their own language or not.

English writing has such leftover letters from the Roman alphabet which are not needed from a strictly linguistic standpoint. These surplus letters are 'c, q(u),' and 'x.'

Everything which 'c' represents could be spelled with an 's' or 'k.' The sound(s) which 'q(u)' stands for could be adequately indicated with a 'kw' or 'k.' Finally, what 'x' spells could be represented with a 'ks' or 'gz.'

Conversely, there are some sounds in English which would be more conveniently represented by additional letters. Actually, Old English (Anglo Saxon) writers had added such characters: "aesc" 'æ' and "eth" 'ð.' to the Roman Alphabet.

Unfortunately, these useful added letters were lost after the Norman invasion. The French-speaking and Latin-writing scribes did not choose to use letters other than those available from the Roman Alphabet.

Most of what linguists could offer regarding mapping sounds to symbols has already been put in place by phonics text authors. They have matched the regular portion of the English vocabulary to contrasts shared by most, not all speakers, of English.

Interestingly, some early pragmatic mappings underlying phonics tests were made by a neurologist and pathologist Samuel T. Orton and his students. Commercial and non-profit organizations have employed the original or revised versions of this. Some examples are found in (Orton-Spalding 2001, Orton-Gillingham 2000, and McCulloch 2000.)

Samples matching sounds to letter or letter patterns (phonograms) and phonograms to sounds occur on website pages of the two Orton references. Such mappings are what are used in implicit phonics and what are taught in explicit phonics. This distinction is outside the scope of my discussion but discussions are available in (Hiskes 1998, and McCulloch 2000.)

ONE SIZE DOESN'T REALLY FIT ALL

Phonics authors and publishers do make major departures from linguistic treatments for commercial reasons. Textbook authors and publishers push a one-size-fits-all set of sound-to-letter correspondences. Such books serve a homogenous and monolithic American English language that does not now, nor never did, exist.

For example, some speakers pronounce 'marry,' 'merry,' and 'Mary,' the same; others pronounce 'cot' and 'caught' or 'pin' and 'pen' alike. I have been told, but have not heard for myself, that some speakers pronounce 'boil,' 'bowl,' and 'ball' the same. Likewise, I have been told that others pronounce 'tire,' 'tower,' and 'tar' alike. Personally, I have heard four of the many attested pronunciations of the word 'wash.'

Obviously, one primer cannot accommodate this great variety of differences among speakers in sound-to-letter correspondences. However, for publishers, there is obviously no profit in creating dozens of varied texts.

It would take many separate textbooks for a perfect sound to graph match. It would take dozens to accommodate most students of the different regional and social dialects of the United States. Also, school boards and teaching staffs are not trained to determine which, text among many, their populations require, if such primers did exist. Even if unlimited funds were available for such an under-taking, further pragmatic considerations remain. When all studies were completed for all the dialects, many studies would be obsolete as well as textbooks based on them.

In addition, more training would be required of teachers to use such dialect-specific texts optimally. Finally, there is the problem of schools that must educate people from different regional and/or social dialect backgrounds within one classroom.

Learning sound and letter correspondences more efficiently does not solve everyone's spelling problems in any case. Homophones remain, which require knowledge of context and meaning for writers to choose among alternatives spelled differently.

There are always the questions: what should be learned, when, how, and in what order? Research in linguistics, education, speech and in other areas related to reading continues. There is a lot about reading which is not known; there are conflicting theories to be tested.

A good starting point is the commentary: "A Synthesis of Research on Reading from the National Institute of Child Health and Human Development." Remarks by author Bonita Grossen (1997) are followed by that year's NICHD Research Center's Bibliography.

A more limited introduction to research is found in Roger Sensenbaugh (2000.) "Phonemic Awareness: An Important Early Step in Learning to Read." It is found in the ERIC Clearinghouse on Reading, English, and Communication Digest #119.

Chapter 2

PONDERING ENGLISH SPELLING

In the early years as a first-year--as well as an advanced-composition--teacher, spelling formed part of grading student writing. Like others before, I noted how many otherwise talented students were handicapped by poor spelling ability.

Ordinary dictionaries are minimally helpful to those who cannot spell well enough to look up the words. (Specialized dictionaries for poor spellers do exist that list entries for words under their most common misspellings.) Spell checkers, despite their many benefits, do not help those who cannot distinguish one homophone from another.

Many students, problem spellers, strain to edit spelling more carefully to pass or to do well in a composition course. Once the course is over, quite a few such students suffer an orthographic relapse. They resume their old habits such as using malapropisms or spelling the wrong members of sets of homophones.

Very few poor spellers are simply lazy; quite a few seem resigned to a life of never quite getting it right. For many, correct spelling may assume a much lower priority than the content of what they are spelling. This exceedingly reasonable priority is often abetted by instructors themselves.

However, acknowledging the correctness of the priority does not obviate a simple fact. Poor spelling detracts from the overall impression of even the most well thought-out essay.

Until acquaintance with the work of two linguists, Smith and Sustakoski's, my personal techniques and frustrations had not differed from other colleagues. Grading on spelling and making students compile lists of their most frequently spelled words does not solve poor spellers' problems.

As mentioned earlier, once outside the composition classroom, old habits return quite quickly. Also, perceptions, traditions and expectations limit what techniques are available in terms of being considered reasonable or responsible.

What if I were to require elementary or middle-school style spelling tests of college students? Would the students be the only critics of the practice?

Colleagues from other departments sporadically complain to members of the English department to which I belong. They are distressed about writing from students who have passed First-Year Composition.

The two most frequent complaints concern incorrect usage and, of course, poor spelling. It would fruitless telling colleagues how empty their classrooms would be if every student who had had any spelling problems were flunked. Likewise, it would strain credulity to hear that many students, who spell poorly, can exercise excellent conceptual and content-learning skills.

Neither position would engender either acceptance or a welcome reception. Either would be perceived as excusing English-Department failure, particularly by the applied science and business faculties. Even in academia, little excuse exists for English teachers' not guarantying that every student who has passed their composition courses can spell.

POOR SPELLING-PERCEPTIONS AND POOR-SPELLING PERCEPTIONS

Returning to an earlier discussion, there are very few teachers of writing who will disagree with the following proposition. Critical thinking and the support of well-thought-out theses are more important skills to learn than being able to spell well. Nonetheless, the spelling prowess of a pupil or an employee affects public relations for the respective school or firm.

Instructors who rate spelling as a low priority often expect that such a minor matter can be taken care of later. Some think that all it ought to take is a little effort on students' parts, provided that they are sufficiently motivated.

Unfortunately, this later learning does not take place for some students for whatever reason. How much of a problem do poor spellers face? Further, what responsibility do educators have in regard to providing spelling instruction for their charges?

Over twenty years ago, there was no doubt in the general public's mind. One of the fruits of a good education was the ability to spell correctly. The elementary and the secondary English teachers had the chief, but not the sole, responsibility for insuring this skill.

At that time, an article in my hometown newspaper reported my remarks on the subject of declining writing levels. The interviewer and I discussed several different areas of concern. However, the sole depiction of error in the illustrations which accompanied the article were reproductions of misspellings (Buyers, 1977, A-8.)

That was a long time ago. Many things have changed since then. Changes in technology alone force many people into a perpetual game of catch up.

Ignoring changes in audio and video playback devices or improvements in telecommunications, computer technology alone places constant demands on technical skill maintenance. Who can be expected to spend time as well on every detail of traditional literacy?

During the years since then, the computer age has affected the office and the classroom as well as many homes. How much should anyone have to edit e-mail?

Anyhow, spell checkers abound. Aren't misspellings less consequential in the e-mail age?

Ken Kister (2000) argues that spelling does matter and that poor spelling damages the credibility of business and professional people. Kister contends that correspondence, reports, news releases etc. need to be correctly spelled.

Additionally, Keith C. Ivey (1998), a technical editor and the webmaster for EEI Communications shares a similar view. He reminds us that the computer screen has not completely replaced print material.

He reminds his readers that computer displays are not as easy to read as ink on paper. Even if people could easily carry computers to the beach, for example, they would still need to worry about sand and recharging. Ivey contends that the printed word will always be with us. Books will continue to exist, even if in an electronic form.

Such business-community reactions imply that extreme predictions of the immanent demise of the obligation to spell correctly may be premature. Societal sanctions do not necessarily vanish in response to technical change.

Marilyn vos Savant writes a regular column for Parade Magazine. On August 13, 2000, her topic was spelling. The column was feature length on this occasion and also merited a front cover. Among many points discussed, vos Savant describes perceptions made about individuals who misspell.

She contends that misspellings evoke strong negative associations among those who read them. The writer who misspells is often perceives as less intelligent or too careless to pay attention to detail.

After mentioning vos Savant's book on spelling (2000), the article claimed that poor spellers are often poorly organized in certain areas of detail. By systemic practice of good habits, attention to details necessary for good spelling will grow. Once this attention moves from conscious striving to habit, poor spellers can become better spellers.

The article held out hope to those who have suffered as a result of their poor spelling. By learning the techniques in her book, vos Savant suggests that anytime is not to late for anyone to start to become a better speller.

Like Kister, cited earlier, vos Savant believes that the credibility of people in professional, commercial, technical, executive etc. positions is damaged by misspellings.

She goes even further in regard to misspellings by teachers. She contends that the public is even affronted if school-teachers misspell, particularly in notes sent home to parents.

Within the academic community itself, such attitudes are also present. Rare occasions of misspellings by English department instructors often meet gloating, as well as disapproval, from colleagues in other departments.

In judging spellers' abilities, spelling plays a role out of proportion to its role in those same spellers' communications. Most people recognize some, if not most, misspelled words. There is a comfortable right and wrong, black and white decision-making process, at least in the public mind.

Spelling is, or was, a shared enterprise for anyone taught in schools before the arrival of often misapplied whole language teaching. An early activity which required some memorization, spelling fell among "musts" like alphabetical order, multiplication tables, telling time and right from left.

A word usually has one or two spellings, one of which may be preferred. Misspellings lack the ambiguous gray shadings typical of judging higher-level error. During their school years, people may have been lauded and rewarded for their own spelling ability or condemned and humiliated by it.

Regardless of which was the case, there is fairly uniform public agreement on the following proposition. High-school and college graduates who cannot spell well have been poorly served by their educational institutions. Consequently, there is a gap between writing-pedagogy priorities and public perception in regard to the importance of spelling.

A disjunction exists between spelling as intellectual and as social marker. Misspelling is not an intellectual, but a social, problem. Misspellers are not intellectually, but socially, handicapped. Thus, parents and employers want schools to address spelling, regardless of how clear or logical or interesting students' written presentations are otherwise.

Spelling's role in achieving literacy is another matter. Decoding a culture's representations of speech is essential to learning how to read.

However, several answers exist to the question: just what should teachers do to help pupils to identify words from what spells them? As mentioned before, differing scholarly and pedagogical opinions regarding optimum means for mastering vocabulary fuels the whole-language versus phonics debate.

Such issues are further complicated by disputes over related concerns. How much does interference from nonstandard syntax and sound systems affect reading? How much class time should be spent in mastering alphabetic mapping versus exposure to varieties of model texts? How gender-neutral, multicultural etc. should or could reading texts be?

This presentation merely touches upon such controversies, important as they are. Instead, the focus is on articulating an alternative spelling perspective, drawn from a technical presentation by Smith and Sustakoski (1965.) Their linguistic perspective, largely overlooked by contemporary linguistics, has elements to evaluate independently of anyone's specific theoretical commitment.

Spelling approaches commonly focus either upon English spelling's irregularities or upon its less obvious regularities. Predominantly, those concerned with effecting literacy more quickly and more broadly consider the spelling system to be too irregular, e.g., Steve Bett (1998.) Bett lengthily discusses the cost to English-speakers in time, money and suffering from our spelling system's poor sound to symbol match.

A. R. Brown (1998) has a lengthy online list of both annotated links and bibliographical references on the subject. The site not only distinguishes approaches for spelling reform into subtypes, but also provides some historical perspective on concerns with English spelling.

Although complaints against "thc" English spelling system abound, there are those who argue that spelling regularity is subtle rather than absent. Raymond Laurita (1991) holds such a view.

He believes that printed English has a limited number of regularly formed categorical groupings. These groupings are hierarchical.

That is, they exist at five distinct levels of difficulty. Each builds upon and incorporates characteristics of the levels below them.

Levin (1999) presents arguments, not included here, for the regularity of most English spelling as well. His particular thrust concerns ESL students.

A NEW LOOK AT AN OLD SUBJECT

Smith and Sustakoski's treatment differs from both "the spelling system" is "very bad" and "not that bad" approaches. Rather than the English spelling "system," they propose the alternative: "systems."

For Smith and Sustakoski, English writing has several co-existent spelling systems. The following adapts, and does not directly render, their work.

This adaptation has FOUR English spelling systems, independent of, but interdependent with, one another. Smith and Sustakoski's work is blended here with what I consider compatible technical linguistic concerns with different terms for overlapping subjects.

Two such terms are phonosymbolism and linguistic iconism, now only beginning to be systematically studied. Scholars have compiled extensive bibliographies, and professional groups of scholars with phonsymbolic interests have formed.

Typical historical explanations for sound changes affecting spelling through pronunciation changes are sound law, analogy, compounding and clipping. These represent most explanations for individual word changes in etymological descriptions. (I will not define these terms as this would replicate facts available in any good History of the English Language text.)

At the periphery of such explanations are words gathered under descriptive names such as 'echoic words, back formations, blends,' and 'folk-etymology.' These number among what have been considered more haphazard, less easily systematized, explanations. These areas have become research sources for phonosymbolism and linguistic iconism.

Pioneer discussions are available in print in Bloomfield (1933), Hill 1958, and Markel and Hamp (1961), Slightly later print sources are Malkiel (1978), Tyma (1978 & 1979), and Westcott (1976, 1979 & 1980.) More recent on-line sources are Branner (1994), Post (1994), Reiner (1994), Gaskell (1998), Kemmer (2000), and Magnus (2000a & 2000b.)

While researching phonosymbolism for other purposes (Hoffman, 1982, 1987 and 1990), I concluded that it had a role in spelling. Familiarity with Smith and Sustakoski's work led me to possible applications through combining insights from phonosymbolism with elements of their treatment. Pedagogical presentations, groupings, and sequencings may be systematized from an entirely new direction.

Besides the concept of multiple, but coexistent, spelling systems, Smith and Sustakoski dealt extensively with third-system vocabulary cell division. Their quite technical treatment will be presented less technically and with illustrative examples. Readers should be aware that cell (morpheme) boundaries in illustrations will not always conform to the words' historical and/or dictionary boundaries.

Each spelling system has a dominant, but usually not exclusive, source vocabulary, requiring a different strategy to spell it. Also, each system has attributes and functions largely or totally exclusive of the others.

Chapter 3

FOUR SYSTEMS

SYSTEM I

The first system is the relic or sight-word vocabulary of English which contains words with silent letters and unique spellings. Some of the most ordinary high and low-frequency English vocabulary from Anglo-Saxon and other Germanic languages occur here.

Smith and Sustakoski (VIII, p. 4) note:

> Such a residual phenomenon ... can be seen [among late period writings] in the Hieroglyphic Egyptian ... , in ... Cuneiform Akkadian, in ... Latin ... and even in Hieroglyphic Maya. High and low frequency lexical forms tend to remain relatively stable in graphic representation, even though their pronunciations may change.

Also, some low-frequency obsolete and poetic English words fit this category. Late additions, by strategy not source, are Greek-origin words with silent letters.

The only spelling strategy for "sight words," is memorization. System I. includes some abbreviations, coined words, acronyms, and spellings unpredictable by regular rules or words with silent letters.

SYSTEM II.

The second system includes regular, primer or ear vocabulary, covering the whole range of English content: the vocabulary of phonics and beginning readers. Long and short vowels, and silent "e" and the most common "spelling rules" apply to this vocabulary. Although Norman French is the dominant source, words from any "regularized" source belong to this vocabulary. Its characteristic spelling strategy is to "sound-it-out" syllable by syllable.

Regularizing or simplifying spelling can include both informal, limited use and formal, general use. Movements from system I into system II. like Lite beer, thruway, donut (doughnought) etc. are examples of the former. Words from system III. can also move into system II. Fantasy (Greek to Latin: phantasia), paper (Egyptian to Greek to Latin: papyrus), and ether (Greek to Latin: aether) illustrate the latter.

SYSTEM III.

Latin and Latinized words have entered English in five separate waves, grouped into the former two and the latter three. Most former group words are regular, reflecting late Latin and early French, while the latter, more classically spelled, are in System III.

Greek words, entering Latin during the classical period, entered English with Latin spellings. Besides Latin and Greek through Latin, The system III also has vocabulary from other Latinized sources. Most system III. vocabulary is technical, including terms for Arts and Sciences, and Theology.

A large, but finite, number of prefixes, suffixes and other parts of these vocabularies combine to make the technical vocabulary. The speller must memorize letters that spell-the-cell: prefixes, suffixes and other word parts (morphemes) that form the word being spelled.

The third system has its own rules, with somewhat different mappings between Latin and Greek, though cells from both are often combined. Such rules and letter to sound mappings often have not received enough attention in schools.

Such purposeful systemic matchings generally are absent in spelling materials but more frequently occur with vocabulary building instead. They are hardly unknown to educators who return to teach them decade after decade.

A sample of such instruction, spread over forty years, include Burliss (1949), Ehrlich (1968), Leuschnig (1982), Danner (1985) and Giagrande (1987.) The first two titles, respectively, are *Latin and Greek in Current Use* and *Instant Vocabulary*. The third example is *Etyma: an Introduction to Vocabulary Building from Latin and Greek*. Last are an *Introduction to an Academic Vocabulary, Word Clusters from Latin, Greek and German*, and *Latin in the Service of English*.

SYSTEM IV.

The fourth and final system, of modern French origin, includes words on cuisine, manners, high-culture and fashion. Usually, one or two syllables, the stressed part requires a combination of two strategies. The initial portion can generally be sounded out; the final must often be memorized.

This system enters many people's passive vocabulary fairly early: bouquet, bureau, filet etc. Many people, aware of this vocabulary's French provenience, are neither French students nor French speakers.

Advertisements for fashion, formal dining, cosmetics and other areas use French-origin names for products and brands. Certain cultural and athletic events as well as some military applications use French vocabulary for some technical terms.

Content-rich multi-media contexts make the meanings clear. Repetition in wider contexts among more speakers in more English-speaking areas permits importation of this vocabulary into the English-speaking mainstream.

David Gelman (1983) writes a satirical article about retaliating against French laws requiring replacement of English words and phrases with French equivalents. He argues until he reaches the point where it is clear that English would be impoverished without its French borrowings. The French imports quite obviously satisfy a genuine need for English speakers.

THE FOUR-SYSTEM FIGURE

The four system figure depicts the systems' respective attributes, functions, origins and strategies, arranged so comparisons can be made at a glance. The most important among the labels listed is strategy.

Many spellers have learned only, and consequently employ only, the first two strategies. The first two strategies serve well enough for systems I. and II., respectively and, when combined, serve for system IV.

This is not the case for system III. Consequently, system III's. spell-the-cell strategy and unrecognized system III. spelling problems constitute the major strategy emphasis of this book.

The presentation order somewhat recapitulates the history. That is, system I.'s dominant vocabulary is earlier than system II.'s dominant vocabulary and so on.

This is a relative, not absolute, difference as any of the four systems may gain new vocabulary. For example, brand names, coined names, acronyms, or new Greek word-cell borrowings may contain silent letters, requiring system I.'s memorization strategy.

The relic vocabulary contains earlier, now obsolete, spellings in the native vocabulary. Regular vocabulary reflects the influence of the Norman Invasion both on vocabulary and spelling from Middle to Early Modern English.

The technical vocabulary from and through Latin came in from the Middle Ages up until the present. Modern French vocabulary is just that: modern.

Much of the information to be presented is not new. What is different is the more systematic use of that information. Which words are better memorized, which words should be sounded out, and what portions of words should be memorized?

To determine which strategy to employ, a speller must be familiar enough with distinguishing characteristics of the respective systems. The following discussions address the issue of the distinctions among the systems in some detail.

Beside distinguishing the systems, substantial examples of applications to the improvement of spelling vocabulary in the third system are included. As may have become apparent, the third system is the most problemsome of all the systems which are addressed.

FOUR ENGLISH VOCABULARIES WHICH REQUIRE FOUR SETS OF SPELLING STRATEGIES.

	Vocabulary I.	Vocabulary II.	Vocabulary III.	Vocabulary IV.
T I T L E.	Relic/Residual Vocabulary/ Sight Words	Regular/ Primer/Ear Vocabulary	Borrowed Latinate/ Eye Vocabulary	Borrowed French Vocabulary
T Y P E S	High and Low Frequency Words, Often with Silent Letters.	Words Follow Common Rules: Long / Short Vowels and Silent E	Technical Words of Arts and Sciences, Philosophy and Theology.	Words of Manners, Culture, Fashion and Cuisine.
S O U R C E S	*Anglo-Saxon,* Low German, Scandinavian; Greek and Others.	*Norman French,* Anglo-Saxon, Low German, Scandinavian and Others through *Nor-French.*	*Latin,* Greek, Arabic and Others through *Latin*	*Modern French* and Others through *Modern French.*

(Italics mark dominant source of origin and/or transmission.)

	Vocabulary I.	Vocabulary II.	Vocabulary III.	Vocabulary IV.
S T R A T E G Y	Memorize	Sound-it-out	Spell-the--cell	Left of Vowel, Sound-it-out, right of Vowel, Memorize

WHAT DOES A FOUR-SYSTEM VIEW GAIN?

To illustrate, how is the consonant-letter cluster "ch" pronounced? Typical treatments say that are three pronunciations for this "blend." From the four-system, four-vocabulary view-point, each spelling system has only one pronunciation.

I. AND	II.	III.	IV.
church,	champion,	chrome, epoch,	chic, chalet,
much,	charge,	chronology,	chateau, crochet,
chill,	march,	chemistry,	penchant,
birch,	chalice.	chasm, stomach,	chagrin,
		chaos.	Chevrolet[tm].

(Chevrolet[tm] is a registered trademark of General Motors Corporation.)

Familiarity and frequency may skew perceptions with words from systems III. and IV. 'stomach' and 'Chevrolet[tm]' are common vocabulary items. 'stomach' does not function as technical but as ordinary vocabulary.

'Chevrolet[tm]' seems neither high culture nor particularly foreign. 'Chevrolet[tm]' and 'stomach' are not atypically spelled but are more commonly used members of vocabularies less commonly used in ordinary conversation.

In these examples, the consistency of a single spelling to sound relationship was demonstrated within respective categories. Additional grasp of the value of the approach is evident in the reverse procedure. That is, how is the same sound or sounds represented in the respective vocabularies?

Going from sound to letters also shows systemic differences in some but not all cases. All four systems regularly use the letter 'f,' single or double, for what linguists call a "labiodental voiceless spirant."

System I., most commonly uses 'f' and '-ff.'   'feet, leaf, fall, if.'
                                                         'cliff, stuff.'

Less commonly, system I. uses '-gh.':   'laugh, cough, rough, tough.'

System II. uses 'f.':	'feast, forest, chief, beef.'
What does system III's	'physics, photoelectric, tele-
Greek part have?	phone, hieroglyph, graph.'
Its Latin part is much like systems	
I. and II., with 'f' and '-ff.'	'filial, sacrifice, pontiff.'
System IV has the expected:	'chef, clef, fete, filet.'

There are two "atypical" spellings. The first is '-gh' in a limited list within system I. The other is 'ph' everywhere within the Greek-origin portion of system III.

There are two subsets in system three but both sets share some cells and combinations with cells from both sets are extremely common in coined scientific terms.

Words either with silent letters or with unpredictable pronunciations fall into system I. vocabulary. The term "Relic" vocabulary may seem somewhat strange when Greek borrowings also qualify for membership.

Why not include all Greek borrowings in System III. since they share common origins? What should the determining factor in assigning a word to one of the four vocabularies. Since the concern here is spelling, not history of the language, the assignments in this presentation are determined by one criterion: strategy.

SOURCE VERSUS STRATEGY

Sometimes a word's strategic assignment can separate it from its etymological relatives whose origin and strategy match. For example, 'think' and 'thought' come from system I.'s Germanic vocabulary.

Yet, anyone can sound out 'think' in system II. without memorization. 'Thought's' silent letters keep it in system I. 'Ptomaine' and 'gnome' are system III. Greek vocabulary in origin, but silent letters make them strategically system I.

System II. versus III. vocabulary may figure in cyclical swings between phonics and its alternative in any era, presently, whole language. System II. vocabulary--'cat, hat, fat; sing, wing, cling; bet, set, get'--suits decoding well. Generations of English-speaking students have been taught by this method for good or ill.

Yet, without creative primer authors, (like Dr. Seuss) home and playground vocabulary can become stale fast. Such words form only a small part of even children's active vocabulary in any case.

Even before PC's, pupils faced phonographs, telephones, chemistry sets, photographs etc. System III. vocabulary confronts them from fourth grade on, waxing geometrically in high-school through college texts.

Pupils limited to system II. vocabulary in texts can spell what bores them, if not tuning out first from lack of interest. Abandoning phonics (decoding) does allow children to learn and use more interesting and varied vocabulary. Yet, multisyllabic system III. vocabulary words pose later problems in reading--and even more, in spelling--for many people.

Balancing advantages and disadvantages between system II. and III. vocabulary supports approaches combining both phonics and whole-language. Stressing only one vocabulary at the expense of the other has possible negative consequences, regardless of which is diminished or excluded.

Teaching literacy by attempting a balance between both concerns is not at all a novel or idiosyncratic idea. Articles suggesting such a balance for reasons related to the above exist in many venues.

Among others John Holdren (1995) wrote an article entitled "Not 'either/or' but 'both/and': Phonics and Whole Language." Among other sources cited, Holdren quotes Professor Connie Juel (1994, p. 136) who sees the phonics versus whole language debate as artificial:

She contends that a children cannot read or write well without having mastered the written code of English. This includes bright, creative and knowledgeable children.

On the other hand, the quality of what children read does matter. Knowing the code does not mean that children will use it in reading or writing unless inspired, for example, by a good story.

Chapter 4

System III.: Spell-the-Cell

Some System III. vocabulary items seem to be good candidates for system II.'s sound-it-out strategy. Even when the sound-it-out strategy is successful, there is more involved than meets the eye or ear. Examples of such covert complexity are words containing the word cell 'nat-,' which roughly means "born.":

nat-ive,	nat-al;
nat-ion,	nat-ion-al;
nat-ure,	nat-ur-al.

Sounding out system III. words often requires violating some of the most common system II. rules. To illustrate this claim requires examining the letters of the cell 'nat' in these words in order.

'N' which has a single value works well for all the words. 'A' stands for both the long and the short 'a' of system II. Yet, 'a' in both 'national' and 'natural' should represent only a long, not a short vowel, by system II. rules.

That is, "A vowel after one consonant after a vowel should be long." (Compare 'later' and 'latter' as well as 'mated' and 'matted.') By ordinary system II. rules, 'national' and 'natural' should be spelled 'nattional' and 'nattural.'

'T' presents problems. 'Natal' and 'native' 't' follows system II. rules. Yet, 'natIon' and 'natIonal' 't,' (either taken alone or with the next vowel) violates system II. mappings. 'Sh.' usually represents their sound in system II. Likewise, the 't' of 'natUre' and 'natUral' violates system II. mapping, which usually represents their sound: 'ch.' (Capitalization in the examples marks letters whose sounds may play a role in 't' representing more than a single pronunciations.)

Some people induce the rules of system III. without formal, conscious instruction. That is, those who have an eye strategy as well as a system II. ear strategy identify themselves inadvertently. They are people who judge whether a system III. word is spelled correctly by whether it "looks right" when it is written.

Cases exist when sound-it-out totally fails system III. vocabulary spellers, and only spell-the-cell works. A loss of similarity in pronunciation often results in a loss of association of meanings among words sharing the same cells.

This is particularly true when a single syllable encompasses a number of word cells. The latter sometimes results from a weak accent on a number of adjacent cells whose pronunciations coalesce. Alternatively, it sometimes results from loss of accent on cells which are accented in one word but not in another.

The regularity of cell spelling in the following list is usually missed, at least, consciously. If anyone could spell the list, more likely, it would be someone who could relate cells and not just memorize words.

Syllable divisions in the examples below are useless for helping spellers sound-them-out. The major cell 'sci' which appears below has three different pronunciations in the examples but has one spelling. Regularity among the examples is opaque when the words are sounded out as syllables, but it becomes transparent when divided by word cells.

Sounding-out masks the shared role of 'sci' in 'science' and 'conscience.' Syllabifying is no help in 'conscience' and 'conscious' as the second syllable lacks enough separately pronounced consonants to reconstruct the spelling.

Rough Definition:	Word Cell Division:	Syllable Division for Most Dialects:	Homophones of '-sci-'
Doing what one knows is right.	con-sci-en- ti-ous "	con-sci-en-tious	"she"
How one knows right from wrong.	" con-sci-en-ce "	con-science	"sh"
State of being able to know,	" con-sci- -ous "	con-scious	"sh"
A way to know.	sci-en-ce	sci-ence	"sigh"

Lack of accent plus some Latin and English sound rules collapse some original Latin consonants into fewer modern English consonants. System III. regularity means little or no change in cell spelling, as shown in the two groupings below. What variation occurs is minimal, and is often predictable.

	-vert	-tain	-mit	-ply	-sist	-spire	-sume
re-	re -vert	re -tain	re -mit	re -ply	re-sist	re -spire	re -sume
con-	con-vert	con-tain	coM-mit	coM-ply	con -sist	con-spire	con-sume
per-	per-vert	per -tain	per -mit		per- sist	per-spire	sub-sume
sub-	sub-vert	suS-tain	sub -mit	suP-ply	sub -sist		
ad-		aT-tain	ad-mit	aP-ply	aS .sist	aS spire	aS-sume

>vert<	>sist<	re-	sub-	Twelve word cells
>tain<	>spire<	con-	ad-	spell twenty-two
>mit<	>sume<	per-	*Prefixes*	words exactly and
>ply<	*Roots*			nine partially

	-port	-ject	-tract	-pel	-pose	pos-it-ion
de-	de -port	de -ject	de -tract		de -pose	de -pos-it-ion
ex-	ex -port		ex -tract	ex -pel	ex -pose	ex -pos-it-ion
pro-		pro -ject	pro -tract	pro-pel	pro -pose	pro-pos-it-ion
in-		in -ject		iM- pel	iM -pose	iM -pos-it-ion
dis-	dis-port	dis -ject	dis -tract	dis-pel	dis -pose	dis -pos-it-ion

>claim<	>pel<	de-	in-	-it	Twelve word cells
>ject<	>pos<	ex-	dis-	-ion	spell twenty-two
		pro-			words exactly and
>tract<	*Roots*		*Prefixes*	*Suffixes*	three partially.

Capitals indicate letters in word cells differing from typical spellings. Italics indicate where a letter's pronunciation differs from the cell's most common pronunciation. Bold indicates an 'e,' which does not spell the cell but signals pronunciation for one or more other letters. There is also a pattern of accents. In all two-syllable verbs listed, the accent falls on the last syllable for most American dialects. In the four-syllable examples, the accent falls on the second to last syllable.)

Greek or Greek and Latin combination patterns can be more complicated.(General Pattern of 1st. " and 2nd. Loudest ' Accent Appears Above Examples.)

		>metr<		-ic		-y
		"	'	"		"
therm-o-	therm-	o-meter	therm-	o-metr-ic	therm-	o-metr-y
bar-o-	bar-	o-meter	bar-	o-metr-ic		"
chron-o-	chron-	o-meter	chron-	o-metr-ic	chron-	o-metr-y
tach-o-	tach-	o-meter	'	"	tach-	o-metr-y
alt-i-	alt-	i-meter	'	"	alt-	i-metr-y
tele-	tel	e-meter	tele-	e-metr-ic	tel	e-metr-y

>metr<	>tach<	tele-	-ic	-o-	Eleven cells spell nine
>therm	>alt<		-y	-i-	poly-syllabic words
>bar<		*Prefix*		*Non-*	perfectly and, six more,
>chron	*Roots*		*Suffixes*	*Finals*	substantially.

		>scop<		-ic		-y
	"	'	'	"		"
kal-eid-o-	kal-eid-	o-scope	kal-eid-	o-scop-ic		"
spectr-o-	spectr-	o-scope	spectr-	o-scop-ic	spectr-	o-scop-y
micr-o-	micr-	o-scope	micr-	o-scop-ic	micr-	o-scop-y
hor -o-	hor-	o-scope	'	"	hor-	o-scop-y
tele	tel	e-scope	tel	e-scop-ic	tel	e-scop-y
peri-	per	i-scope	per	i-scop-ic		

>kal<	>micr<	-o-	tele-	-ic	Eleven cells spell
>eid<	>hor<		peri-	-y	fifteen polysyllabic
>spectr<	>scop<	*Non-*			words perfectly.
Roots		*Final*	*Prefixes*	*Suffixes*	

		>graph< " '		-er "		-y " '		-ic "
phon-	phon-	o-graph	phon-	o-graph-er	phon-	o-graph-y	phon-	o-graph-ic
phot-	phot-	o-graph	phot-	o-graph-er	phot-	o-graph-y	phot-	o-graph-ic
pict-o-	pict-	o-graph	"		pict-	o-graph-y	pict-	o-graph-ic
mon-	mon-	o-graph	mon-	o-graph-er			mon-	o-graph-ic
aut-o-	aut-	o-graph	"		aut-	o-graph-y	aut-	o-graph-ic
bi-o-	"	'	bi-	o-graph-er	bi-	o-graph-y	bi-	o-graph-ic
tele-	tel	e-graph	tel	e-graph-er	tel	e-graph-y	tel	e-graph-ic

>phon<	>phot<	-er	tele-	-o-	Twelve cells spell
>aut<	>pict<	-y			24 polysyllabic
>bi<	>mon<	-ic			words perfectly.
>graph<				Non-	
Roots		*Suffixes*	*Prefix*	*Final*	

Sometimes spelling patterns shared by system III. Greek and Latin vocabulary follow sound patterns which transcend particular cell boundaries. Such patterns may ultimately cause unconscious reanalysis by native speakers, thus creating new cell divisions, not in the original languages.

Greek	Latin	Greek	Latin	
aut-o"-ma-t-is'-m	leg-it"-im-is'-m	char"-is'-m*	an"im-is'-m	nouns
aut-o"-ma-t-is'-t	leg-it"-im-is'-t		an"im-is'-t	nouns
aut"-o-ma-te'	leg-it"-im-ate'	char"-is-m-ate'	an"im-ate'	verbs
	leg-it"-im-ate		an"im-ate	adjective
aut'-o-ma-t"-ic		char'-is-m-at"-ic		adjective
aut'-o-ma-t"-ion	leg-it'-im-at"-ion	char'-is-m-at"-ion	an'im-at"-ion	nouns
		char-is"-ma*	an"im-a	nouns
		* alternatives		

Speakers of English and related languages are generally unaware of the unique and usually unrecognized resource and paradox of empty intersections. I refer to the empty intersections of Latin (sometimes Greek) word cells as in the two lists above. Heirs and borrowers of these cells can spell, pronounce, and even guess, word meanings which do not now, but could, exist.

Classical Latin and Greek are dead languages, but their cells endure in modern languages which have either descended or borrowed from them. Moreover, their word cells continue in the technical discourse of speakers of English, related European, and even unrelated languages.

Latin and Greek cells exist not only in inherited words, but also in words coined from novel combinations of original cells. For example, 'Genome' and 'electrolytic' are not inherited words themselves, but they do contain inherited cells.

LEARNING SYSTEM III. IN PATTERNS

System III. words can be taught other than in isolation or in the context of reading and writing. Besides the two illustrations above of two-cell pairings, there are other more complex patterns which are possible. Some examples follow.

The examples that are provided below are fairly rough. There are more blank than filled spaces. Someone with better pedagogical training could probably provide a tighter and more productive set of examples. However, the examples do support the efficiency of spelling the cell.

The students need to see word-cell repetition in two separate contexts. They need to see not only that word cells are minimally variant and occur repeatedly in many combinations. They also need to be made aware that the patterns or sequences in which cells occur are often repetitive as well.

Learning the spelling of a single pattern opens up the possibility of spelling all the words that share that pattern. To learn a new word in the pattern does not mean learning all the new letters in the word, but only the letters of the new cell.

If that spelling is already known, no letters need be memorized. All that is needed is to recognize that one cell substitutes for another in an already familiar pattern. Much can be spelled from little.

The crossover point for many poor spellers of system III. vocabulary is not learning to spell, but to recognize, new words. I believe many people are unaware of this paradox.

More precisely, most people already know letters for spelling cells in system III. words which they do not know. That is, they already know the letters for the cells which they have to spell. What they have not learned is to segment system III. words into recognizable cells because they are still working with letters alone.

Thus, in most cases, people need to recognize what cells occur in what sequence in a new system III. word. Once the cells and their sequence are known, the spelling of the word is usually known.

System III. cells--not letters--directly spell words. Most cells (when accented or isolated) can be sounded out or easily memorized. Exceptions are Greek cells with silent letters or with patterns very different from system II.

The illustration below reads both from top down and from left to right. It shows that different cells can attach strings of identical cells. Only what differs needs to be learned as new. Much of what is spelled in system III. are repeated cells and/or repeated strings of cells.

```
                              sent
                               /
            de                 i
              \                /
        com - part – ment - al – iz (s) – at – ion
          /                  / |   |  \
          a                 ly it  e  m, t
                             |
                             y
```

The word cells to follow are labeled without any formal definitions. The patterns use six columns and thirteen rows to present some common repetitive patterns which English has available in system III.

More intersections are empty than are filled. However, the number of polysyllabic words which are spelled is about double the number of cells which are needed to spell them.

Seventeen word cells form 39 words of varying length.

*Two his-torically distinct 'ment' cells form like patterns.	Prefixes:	Inflecting Suffixes:	Other Suffixes:	Non-final:	Roots:
	a-				>ment<*
	com-	=ed	-al	-i-	>part<
	de-	=ing	-at		>sent<
			-ion		
			-it		
			-iz (s)		
			-ly		
			-ment*		
			-y		

		part=ing	a
		part=ed	b
		part	c
sent-i-ment			d
sent-i-ment-al-it-y	ment-al-it-y		e
sent-i-ment-al	ment-al		f
sent-i-ment-al-ly	ment-al-ly		g
sent-i-ment-al-ize			h
sent-i-ment-al-iz-at-ion			i
sent-i-ment-al-is-m	ment-al-is-m		j
sent-i-ment-al-is-t	ment-al-is-t		k
sent-i-ment-al-iz=ing			l
sent-i-ment-al-iz=ed			m

de-part=ing			a
de-part=ed			b
de-part		a-part	c
de-part-ment	com-part-ment	a-part-ment	d
			e
de-part-ment-al	com-part-ment-al	a-part-ment-al	f
de-part-ment-al-ly	com-part-ment-al-ly		g
de-part-ment-al-ize	com-part-ment-al-ize		h
de-part-ment-al-iz-at-ion	com-part-ment-al-iz-at-ion		i
de-part-ment-al-is-m			j
			k
de-part-ment-al-iz=ing	com-part-ment-al-in=ing		l
de-part-ment-al-iz=ed	com-part-ment-al-iz=ed		m

The patterns above do not result from exhaustive pedagogical research. Careful research should uncover many more productive patterns. Further, people--more knowledgeable and experienced in elementary and secondary pedagogy than I am--certainly could design more student-friendly patterns.

What I have included are rudimentary illustrations which, when improved, may lead to pedagogical presentations for enhancing instruction in spelling system III. vocabulary. For additional information, I presented and labeled individual word cells whose combinations make up the words in the illustrations.

For pedagogy, should word cells be analyzed and identified as in the examples? This depends on both teachers' and learners' prior experience. Presenting patterns without either analyses or labels is a possible option.

What sort, how many, what sequences are best? I do not have the answers. These are questions for research to determine.

English spelling, viewed as more than one system, opens new avenues for spelling research. Also, it provide a vehicle to reexamine earlier research.

The following pattern uses eight columns and nineteen rows to show some common system III repetitive patterns. Again, more intersections are empty than filled. As before, the number of correctly spelled polysyllabic words amounts to twice the number of cells which are needed to spell them.

The sequencing of the words in these illustrations is not based on any particular linguistic principle. I simply experimented, hit and miss, to find the clearest means to depict the shared elements among the words in the rows and in the columns.

Prefixes:		Non-Final:	Roots:	Inflecting Suffixes:		Other Suffixes:		
circum-	in-	-i-	>cid<		-able		-al	-an
con-	pre-		>cis<	=ed	-er		-ion	-is
de-	ex-			=ing	-ive		-ly	-m
un-					-ness		-or	-t

Twenty-four cells make patterns for forty-eight words.

				a
				b
				c
				d
				e
circum-cis=ed				f
circum-cis=ing				g
circum-cise	con-cise*		pre-cise	h
	con-cise-ness		pre-cise-ness	i
	con-cise-ly		pre-cise-ly	j
circum-cis-ion	con-cis-ion		pre-cis-ion	k
			pre-cis-ion-al	l
			pre-cis-ion-is-m	m
			pre-cis-ion-is-t	n
			pre-cis-i-an	o
			pre-cis-ive	p
				q
				r
				s

	in-cis-or-y		a
	in-cis-or		b
		de-cid-er	c
		de-cid-ed-ness	d
		de-cid-ed-ly	e
ex-cis=ed	in-cis=ed	de-cid=ed	f
ex-cis=ing	in-cis=ing	de-cid=ing	g
ex-cise	in-cise	de-cide	h
			i
			j
ex-cis-ion	in-cis-ion	de-cis-ion	k
		de-cis-ion-al	l
			m
			n
			o
	in-cis-ive	de-cis-ive	p
	in-cis-ive-ness	de-cis-ive-ness	q
	in-cis-ive-ly	de-cis-ive-ly	r
ex-cis-able			s

		A rigorous word cell descrip-
	a	stion on earlier pages
	b	require more explanations.
	c	Among them would be the
un-de-cid-ed-ness	d	reasons why the asterisked
un-de-cid=ed-ly	e	forms is an adjective and why
	f	it ends in an 's,' not 'z'
	g	sound. 'Decided' sometimes,
	h	and 'undecided' usually, func-
	i	tion as adjectives. In such
	j	cases, and in the larger pat-
	k	terns, the '-ed' suffix may not
	l	be inflecting. It may be an
	m	other kind of suffix, identi-
	n	cal in form: '-ed.'
	o	
in-de-cis-ive	p	
in-de-cis-ive-	q	
in-de-cis-ive-ly	r	
	s	

Page size permits only so many rows and columns to be conveniently listed. Much larger patterns could be designed in spread sheets and presented on posters.

There has been no attempt here to deal with either word or cell frequency. Patterns designed with pedagogy in mind could include such considerations

The strategy of how to spell system III. vocabulary is crucial, even if some of its members can be sounded out. Learning a hundred cells is easier than sounding out a thousand system III. vocabulary words.

This idea is hardly original as the two following titles from Raymond Laurita (1991a & 1991b) indicate. The first title is *Spelling Keys to One Thousand One Words from Ten Greek Based Roots.* The second is *Spelling Keys to One Thousand Words from Ten Latin Based Roots.*

Viewing cells another way, regularities occur in differently pronounced system III. vocabulary words e.g.,. 'case' (event) and 'cas-u-al.' In each example, the word-cell is spelled the same although pronounced differently.

'Casual' and 'case' have different 's' pronunciations. 'Casual' has a short rather than long vowel as in 'case' which violates a system II. rule. "It should be long since only a single consonant plus vowel follows it."

'Casual' is also useful to contrast with 'causal' to compare strategies for "letters spell words" models of English spelling. The two words might be spelled by system II.'s sound-it-out strategy, but pose a problem for system III.'s memorization strategy.

The order of 'us/su' could tax some people's memories. System III.'s strategy would emphasize cell identification: 'case' and 'cas-u-al,' 'cause' and 'caus-al.' Teaching correspondences in meaning among differently pronounced--but similarly or identically spelled--cells is central to system III.'s spell-the-cell strategy.

Chapter 5

SYSTEM BUMPING INTO SYSTEM

System III. will be discussed again after considering interference between vocabularies. For example, compare 'cat' and 'kitt-en.'

Both words have the same cell with one difference in pronunciation: short 'a' in 'cat' is replaced by short 'I' in 'kitten.' (Also, compare these modern and archaic counterparts: 'cow-s'
'ki-ne'.

Fortunately, 'cat' and 'kitten' can be sounded out with system II. rules, spelled easily enough to justify sacrificing the word-cell connection. If 'kitten' preserved its spelled connection to 'cat,' it would end up 'citten.'

However, the dominant II. system requires that any 'c' before 'i, e,' or 'y' must be pronounced like 's,' not like 'k.' 'Citten' would wind up pronounced as if it were spelled 'sitten.'

Another model for independence with interdependence, perhaps interference, occurs below with the cell '-voc- i.e. "call."

Call upon	in-voc-at-ion	in-voke
Call back	re-voc-at-ion	re-voke
Call forth	pro-voc-at-ion	pro-voke
Call together	con-voc-at-ion	con-voke

No Roman used 'k' in these cells. Yet, system II. rules stop 'c' before 'e' sounding like 'k,' so alien 'k' has invaded system III. vocabulary.

If all words followed the rules of the vocabulary of their origin, spelling English would be easier. If vocabulary in any one or more of the systems had regularized spellings completely, spelling would be easier. Unfortunately, neither occurred completely.

People, generally unaware of the history of their own language, make sense out of what they have at the time. People tend to lose sight of cells' relationships when respective pronunciations differ due to various processes of sound change.

Likewise, cells and words which are different in origin, but similar in meaning and in pronunciation, are perceived as related. Over time, social perception of spelling, a cachet, may also influence how words are spelled. Consequently, words which start out in one vocabulary may end up in another, or even wander back and forth among the systems.

"Rime of the Ancient Mariner," has 'rhyme' spelled for system II. vocabulary. Both 'rhyme' and 'rhythm,' from Greek via Latin, are system III. vocabulary candidates. 'Rhyme' had many spellings: 'rime (regular); rhime, ryme, rhyme.'

The last spelling was the preferred literary form through all periods, and 'rhythm' occurred in as many forms. In some speakers, the 'th' was lost, leading to periods where the meanings of both intertwined. The Latinate spellings survived, putting both in system III. vocabulary.

Oddly, some words from Norman French had already lost unpronounced double letters from Latin. If they had stayed such, they would have joined their system II. vocabulary sound-it-out kindred. Somewhere, on route, older Latinate spellings were restored, returning them to system III. vocabulary.

Sometimes, spellings vary between systems I. and II. 'Draft' and 'plow' have replaced 'draught' and 'plough' in all uses in the U.S. However, the latter forms still occur for some meanings in Britain.

The changing of the spelling of individual words over time may affect system membership and hence the strategy for spelling those words. Examples of the histories of many different words illustrate this.

Sometimes, routes from original to present vocabulary are unpredictable. 'Isle' and 'island' are clearly - system III. vocabulary. 'Isle's' three-letter word cell has a system II.-rule final 'e' making the 'I' long before the cluster: 'sl.' Island appears to be: 'isl + land' with an 'l' lost like the 't' in 'eighteen' i.e. 'eight + teen' = 'eighteen.' Oddly enough, 'isle' and 'island' have unrelated origins. 'Island' is originally from system I. vocabulary. Anglo-Saxon had the word 'īg' which meant "island" which was identified with 'ēa-land' which meant "water land."

By Middle English, it was spelled 'īland' (length marks are editorial.) If no one had identified it with 'isle,' it would now be in vocabulary II.

Meanwhile, Latin for "island" was 'in-sul-a' It came into English through system II. vocabulary early French as 'isle.'
The problem was that the 's' ceased to be pronounced although it remained in the spelling. This would make it a candidate for system I. vocabulary because of the silent 's.'

'Isle' and 'island' sounded alike and meant the same: the 15th. century linkage was easy as an earlier spelling 'isleland' reflects. Perhaps, pairs like 'mount/mountain,' 'eve/evening,' and 'morn/morning' were involved as the shorter word seems more poetic.

'Island' began in system I. vocabulary, became system II., and ended in system III. vocabulary. 'Isle' began in system III. vocabulary but became system II. vocabulary. It was spelled as system I. vocabulary, but returned to system III. vocabulary where it began.

BORROWED MORE THAN ONCE

The same Latin-origin word cells can appear in systems II., III., and IV vocabularies together—though sometimes altered. The words below are assigned strategically as follows:

MEDICAL	COMMERCIAL or CIVIC	PERSONAL
I.	hot-el	
II.	host-el, host, host-ess	host, host-ess
III.	hosp-it-al hosp-ice		hosp-it-al-it-y

'Host, hostess,' and 'hotel,' are likely system II. vocabulary. Unaccented syllables in 'hostel, hospital' and 'hospice' likely make them system III. vocabulary. Word-cells of common origin can cross vocabularies.

Latin 'hospitare' originally meant "receiving a guest." Derivatives like 'hosp-it-al' associated with knights hospitallers meant "to welcome and harbor strangers."

Its earlier range was more general than its contemporary uses. For several centuries, the early meaning "hotel" alternated with two others.

One was "charitable institution" like an asylum or school for the poor, and the other was today's "medical treatment facility." 'Hostel' and 'hot-el' are cognates with the original meaning; 'hos-pice,' which also meant "inn," has more recently acquired its medical use.

Modern words have divided among the medical, commercial and personal realms. Yet, the use of 'guest'--instead of 'customer, patron' etc. in hotels--betrays its shared origin with one's 'guest' at home. Likewise, 'hostess' occurs with both domestic and commercial uses.

RESHAPING THROUGH REINTERPRETATION

Cross referencing word cells can occur within the same vocabulary. An interesting correspondence can be built using alcohols from the alkane series in organic chemistry.

'Alk-ane' is composed of two word cells, outside the scope of discussion. The words below belong to this series. The laboratory and commercial names for the alcohols are different but equivalent.

Laboratory				Commercial				
	eth-	an-	ol		eth-	yl	alc-	oh-	ol
	meth-	an-	ol		meth-	yl	alc-	oh-	ol
is- o-	prop-	an-	ol	is- o-	prop-	yl	alc-	oh-	ol

The identical cells mean the same thing. 'An' in the first group is equivalent to the 'alc' in the second group. Discussion of the 'yl' and 'oh' will be taken up later.

'Eth-yl' is a combination from Greek 'aith-er,' "eth(er)" and from Greek 'hyl-,' "wood," specifically, or "matter," generally. 'Meth-yl' combines Greek 'meta'—a preposition or prefix with several meanings, here "by means of,"—with the 'yl' from Greek 'hyl-.'

'Alc-oh-ol' is from Arabic 'al-koh'l,' not Latin. The 'al' was the definite article, and 'koh'l' "a mineral used for eyeshadow obtained through distillation."

Later, in Europe, it meant "the process of distillation." Finally, it meant "distilled spirits." Despite origin, speakers sort borrowed cells or words, out of awareness, into one or more of the four vocabularies.

Speakers' associations and perceptions reshape cells e.g. 'alcoholic' divides into system III. cells: 'alc-oh-ol-ic.' Yet, popularly, 'alcoholic,' is perceived as "alcohol" and "one addicted to."

This has spawned 'choc-oholic' and 'work-oholic' where the first cell is a metonym for the whole word 'alK-oh-ol,' 'choC-ol-ate,' 'worK.' The '-oholic' means "addicted to." Each initial cell's ends in a 'k' sound as capitals indicate.

The words 'alcohol' and 'chocolate' break into nice system III. Latinate cells, but—as noted before—'alcohol' comes from Arabic. 'Chocolate' likely comes from Nahuatl (Aztec) 'chocolatl' through Spanish where it acquired its Latin look. 'Work' is native, not borrowed.

A Latin (System III.) look for words borrowed from non-European languages like Native American or Semitic languages is not rare. Arabic, for example, has given English quite a few system III. vocabulary words. Terms in astronomy and mathematics include many borrowings from Arabic.

Less technical English also has Arabic loanwords like admiral from 'amīr al bahr': "ruler/commander of the sea." The Oxford English Dictionary (OED) editors speculate that speakers associated an early spelling 'amiral' with the Latin verb 'adīmrāri': "to wonder."

Now, 'ad-mir-al,' a naturalized system III. word, is indistinguishable from a native Latin borrowing. People, without conscious awareness of Latin word-cells or of borrowings' non-Latin origins, refashion them, nonetheless, into comfortable and familiar patterns.

Word cells (more technically called morphemes) serve a variety of functions. One of the most common functions is to express either referential or grammatical meanings.

Some word cells in system III., however, do nothing but connect meaningful word cells together. A list of more common connecting cells include all vowels: 'o, u, e, i, a' and others outside of the discussion.

As mentioned before, the Arabic 'oh' segment is left over from the Latinate division, 'alc-oh-ol,' and 'yl' is from Greek 'hyl-.' Infrequent among other cells, they are possibly reanalyzable as variant spellings of '-o-' and '-il' of Greek and Latin origin respectively.

Usually, 'il' and 'ul' stay with the same cell which precedes them, for example, 'fam-il-y, fam-il-i-ar.' Sometimes, they do not, for example, 'sim-il-e' and 'sim-il-ar,' but 'sim-ul-t-an-e-ous.' and 'sim-ul-t-an-e-it-y.'

BORROWINGS SPELLED IN TWO SYSTEMS

Sometimes words with related cells are spelled by short forms in system II. and long forms in III. There are several cases where a final 'le' may hide a cell, explicit in a longer form.

Compare 'muscle' and 'mus-c-ul-ar,' where the same short-system II and long-system III occurs. This alternation does not always occur.

Compare 'mob-ile' and 'mob-il-it-y.' Language varieties differ regarding this short-long shift. British English has 'stab-ile,' not 'stable,' alternating with 'stab-il-it-y.'

II. Sound-it-out		III. Spell-the-cell		
table	tab	-ul	-ar	
tablet	tab	-ul	-ate	
fable	fab	-ul	-ous	
stable	stab	-il	-it	-y
	stab	-il	-ize	
able	ab	-il	-it	-y

These borrowed 'le' spellings conceal an 'il' or 'ul.' However, the 'le' in native words like 'bottle' or 'little' represents only the unaccented vowel plus 'l' sounds. Learning word cells instead of memorizing or sounding -out is very productive in situations like the following:

PART-	ic-le	part-IC-ul-ar	The long form has the accented
VEH-	ic-le	veh-IC-ul-ar	vowel to spell the short form's
SPECT-	ac-le	spect-AC-ul-ar	unaccented vowel.

Sounding-out 'infinite' fails to help spell the latter 'i's,' but linked to 'finite,' their spelling is predictable. Sounding-out 'mental' could yield 'mentle' or 'mentile,' but relating 'ment-al-it-y' to 'mental' works.

Thus, unstressed vowels do not always have to be memorized. If one cell is related to another by spelling and meaning, a stressed counterpart enables and unstressed vowel's recovery. This presumes that the speller is aware of the shared word-cell identity despite the pronunciation differences.

Generally, vocabulary I.'s silent letters must be memorized, but sometimes they have spoken kin in vocabulary II. Rarely, vocabulary I.'s silent letters are recoverable by system III. rules if the cells considered have high, if not vocabulary-III. level, consistency.

	tw o		The native cell 'twen,' meaning "two," is not quite as regular as vocabulary III. cells The 'n' is lost in half. the examples and the vowel shows great va-
	tw e	-lve	riation, Yet, the 'tw' cluster occurs in all, making
	tw en	-ty	the 'w' of 'two' a word-cell spelling rather than a
	tw i	-ce	typical vocabulary I. silent letter.
	tw in		
	twain		
be-	tween		
be-	tw i	-xt	
	tw I ne		(Thread or string of two [or more] strands.)
	tw i	-light	
	tw i	-ll	(Weft threads pass over one and under two [or more] threads of the warp in a weave.)
	tw i	-st	(To wind two [or more] strands or threads together--one of several meanings.)

OTHER SYSTEM III. RULES

System III. rules alter certain letters ending Latin/Greek pre-fixes because of consonants which they precede, mostly by Latin, not English, rules. The rules presented below account for variation among three of the most common English-from-Latin prefixes.

con- (together, with, along- side of)	con-flict, con-greg-ate, con-join, con-spire,
/ (not) in- < \ (into)	in-dec-ent, in-frequ-ent in-sens-it-ive, in-cur, in-fer, in-spire, in-stall, in-ter,
ad- (to, toward, against)	ad-dress, ad-junct, ad-here, ad-mire, ad-verse.

(n_1 includes the 'n' of 'con-' and both meanings of 'in-'.)

$n_1 \to$	l before l, r before r	col-late, il-leg-al, il-lum-in-ate, cor-rect, ir-reg-ul-ar, ir-rig-ate,
m before b, m & p.		com-mand, im-poss-ib-le, im-bue,

(Treating 'n' common to both prefixes contradicts Latin history, where 'com' not 'con' is basic. There is a difference between the two prefixes before vowels and 'h'; however, this difference has few or no negative spelling consequences.)

d -->	c before k, q & c,	ac-count, ac-cuse, ac-know-ledge ac-quaint, ac-quire, ac-qui-es-ce,
f before f,		af-fair, af-firm, af-front, af-fect
g before g,		ag-grand-ise, ag-grav-ate, ag-gres-ive
l before l,		al-loc-ate, al-loy, al-lus-ion
n before n,		an-nounce, an-not-ate, an-noy
p before p,		ap-pear, ap-plaud, ap-ply, ap-prove
r before r,		ar-range, ar-rest, ar-rive, ar-rog-ant
s before s,		as-sault, as-scribe, as-sent, as-sert
t before t,		at-tain, at-tend, at-tempt, at-tract

'D' drops before 'sp, st' and 'sc.' However, it is not included in the above list because it is not particularly useful in a spelling application.

'Acknowledge's' 'k' resembles a linguistic fossil as no one now pronounces 'k' in 'knowledge.' 'Ac-' seems to have been prefixed when 'k' was still pronounced, but the historical facts are otherwise.

'Ac-know-ledge' is from original Anglo-Saxon 'on-cn~w-an' which had not yet added '-ledge.' The 'n' of 'on-' was lost, leading to spellings like 'a-know' or 'o-know,' later 'ac-know' by analogy with Latin borrowings. In the 16th. century, 'Ac-know-l-edge' came in.

The 'c' before 'c' rule works even where Latin's descendants lost the 'k' sound before front vowels. Examples where (c = k) precedes (c = s) are 'accede, accent, accept, access, and accident.' Front vowels are made by the tongue tip at the front of the mouth.

The largely Roman-letter list which English inherited represents them by 'i' and 'e' alone or combined with other vowel letters. In words of Greek origin, 'y' alone may also function this way: 'cyan-ide, cycle, cyclone, Cyprus, cylinder, cynic, cypress' etc.

The first of the two 'c's' retains the 'k' pronunciation inherited from Latin. The system II. rule about pronouncing 'c' is historically Latin, not English.

The rule has 'c' pronounced as 'k'--not only before the back-vowel letters 'a, o' and 'u'--but also before consonants. Thus, words like 'accede' and 'accept' reflect aspects both of origin and actual pronunciation.

Some words seem to violate the rule: 'd' to 'c' before 'c.' Examples are 'ascend, ascetic' and 'ascertain,' but 'ascend's' historical word-cell division is not 'as-cend' but 'a-scend;' compare 'de-scend.'

'Ascetic' historically divides as 'asce-t-ic,' not 'as-cet-ic,' perhaps the modern perception. 'Ascertain' likely reflects Middle French: 'assertain.' In all above cases, 's' reflects a pronounced 's,' but all 'c's replacing 'd's are pronounced 'k.'

DIMINISHING RETURNS

For small lists, it may be better for spellers to ignore cell linkage and simply memorize. The list below has few everyday words, e.g. 'symbol, system, sympathy, syndicate, synonym, syllable, symmetry.' Is system III.'s spell-the-cell approach more productive than simple system I. memorization?

'Syn-' from Greek is similar in meaning to Latin "con-"; n_2 refers to "n" of "syn-".)

syn-	syn-apse, syn-dic-ate, syn-erg-y, syn-o-nym,
n_2 --> l before l,	syl-lab-le, syl-lab-us, syl-log-is-m,
m before b, m & p,	sym-bol, sym-metr-y, sym-path-y,
s before s + vowel.	sys-sarc-os-is (a few very technical words)
lost before z or s +	sy□-stal-ic, sy□-stem, sy□-zyg-y,
consonant.	

In any case, to use the rules, one must be able to recognize the hidden 'con-, ad- , in- (into),' and 'syn- (?)' prefixes. The 'in- (not)' prefix should be easily enough identified in words like il-log-ic-al, il-leg-it-im-ate, ir-rat-ion-al, ir-re-fut-ab-le, im-mor-al, im-piet-y etc.

WHERE SPELL-THE-CELL FAILS

System III.'s many regularities do not mean that none but apparent spelling problems exist. Looking at system III. as separate from II. implies the possibility of misdiagnosed spelling problems.

System III.'s usual rule is invariant or minimally different cell spelling, sometimes with a few last-consonant changes, regardless of the pronunciation changes.

However, the system III. vocabulary words below violate that rule. Consequently, there are spelling problems that are not really the result of silent letters, indistinct vowels, or homonyms.

Shorter Form:	main-tain	pro-noun-ce
Longer Form Predicted by Rule:	main-tain-an-ce	pro-noun-ci-at ion
Actual Long: Form	main-t e n-an-ce	pro-n u n-ci-at-ion

Misspellers do not fail to sound-out the words, but unaware, correctly follow a rule which fails them.

Likewise, 'Pro-ced-ure,' a system III. word, should match 'pro-cede,' but is actually spelled 'pro-ceed,' which anomaly occurs in 'suc-ceed' and 'ex-ceed' too. 'Cede' for 'ceed' errors are unrelated to sounding -out.

'Sede, cede, seed, ceed, sead, cead' could all spell-the-cell from a system II. perspective. People misspell '-ceed' words because correctly applying the system III. rule produces '-cede,' which--in these three cases--is incorrect.

Silent letters are sometimes blamed for misspellings when a rule or pattern violation is the more likely culprit.

de- ceive	de-cep-t-ion	de-cei -t
re- ceive	re-cep-t-ion	re-cei*-t
con-ceive	con-cep-t-ion	con-cei -t

Omitting the 'p' of 're-ceiP-t' more likely results from a pattern violation than a missing silent letter. A third column of either no 'p's' or all 'p's' would satisfy system III.

MEANING SHIFTS

Nothing bars shifts in meanings of the cells themselves from original donor-language meanings.

In this presentation's conclusion, examples of intentional standardizing shifts in cell meanings by the scientific community occur. However, some shifts of meaning appear to be unintentional.

Below, a couple of examples of the latter appear. I have chosen cells which are fairly common in use, or are, at least, familiar to most American readers. 'Graph' in words like 'poly-graph, pict-o-graph,' but most clearly in 'graph-ite,' initially meant write.

Now, linked in 'charts' and 'graphs,' most people interpret the cell as "something to see" like 'pict' and 'glyph.' Unhappily, this perceptual shift obscures metaphors in words like 'phot-o-graph' and 'phon-o-graph,' i.e. "writing by light" and "writing by sound."

'Stere' in 'stere-o-phon-ic' was first likely intended to mean "image by sound." Most words including 'stere' such as 'stere-o-type' do reflect the meaning: "image."

Yet, 'mono-phon-ic,' "one (speaker)" exists and the Latin-Greek hybrid, 'quadr-a-phon-ic,' "four (speakers)." These numerical associations pretty much compel an analyst to gloss the 'stere' of 'stereo-phonic' as "two."

That two speakers are required for a stereophonic sound system may adequately explain the shift of meaning from "image" to "two." Yet, I wonder whether 'stere-o-scope-s,' were still in attics, basements and some people's living memories when stereophonic sound arrived.

This instrument was used for recreation and for entertainment. It required two pictures and two lenses, for three-dimensional effects.

Chapter 6

PROBLEMS FROM FLAWED
OR ABSENT EXPLANATIONS

Final silent E's frequent and emphasized appearance in text-books looks like a press agent's dream. People could easily draw the conclusions that most final e's are silent.

Final 'e's' are a good place to compare vocabularies. Even regular vocabulary II, has several final varieties:

The most familiar is the silent 'e' which spells nothing but marks the preceding vowel as long:

'make, cede, rite, code, fume.'

There are one-syllable words where 'e' marks the long vowel:

'be, he, me, she, we.'

Final 'e' can mark prior consonant, not vowel length, value: solace, surface.'

'allege, college, crevice, notice, cottage, courage;

Vocabulary IV. has some pronounced final "e's," some retaining French accents in words of two or more syllables. Such vocabulary IV. final "e's." include:

'applique, attaché, cafe, cliche, consommé, passe, résumé, reveille*, risqué, roue.'

Some spellings of word ends which do not follow system II. rules are from vocabulary III. Examples are:	'acme, agape*, anemone, epitome, finale, recipe, sesame. hyperbole, Nike[tm].'

(Nike[tm] is a registered trademark of Nike Inc.)

Some loans from Spanish/ Amerindian via Spanish, fit system I. (memorizables), not II.:	'adobe, Apache, Chile, Commanche, padre*, Don Quixote.'

* The final '-e' of 'agape,' system III., and 'padre,' system I., keeps the donor languages' closest English match, the rest usually anglicized. Conversely, final '-e' of 'reveille,' system IV., is anglicized. The rest of system IV vocabulary usually keeps the closest English match to the French.

Other system I. final 'e's' include functionless,* which have no vowel pronunciation, mark no vowels long and affect no preceding consonant.	'above, dove (bird), come, some; done, one; glove, love, shove; have, give, live (verb).'

(*'No function' may be an exaggeration, e.g. '-ve' may just spell the final 'v' sound in all four vocabularies.)

Final '-e' examples above, would appear simply a large class of exceptions to "regular" spelling rules if only one spelling system is invoked. Cornell Kimball (2nd entry), reviews a book (Ramsden 1993) which recommends studying Greek and Latin roots, for spelling improvement.

Kimball faults Ramsden for basing a model of spelling on unchanging word cells and simple rules for adding affixes. Kimball argues that there are still too many exceptions.

Kimball concludes that the only way for Ramsden's method to be reliable is for there to be no exceptions. Since there are exceptions, the rules do not spare us from lists of exceptions like those in traditional spelling methods.

With multiple spelling systems assumed, some items once taken as exceptions are shown to belong to classes. Exceptions decrease if analogy pressures words from systems I. and III. to become spelled in system II.

Plurals are a good place to examine this. The following two sets of comparisons show the pressure of the regular system on plurals of both native and borrowed vocabularies.

The first set of comparisons deals with the 'f' > 'v' plurals which have decreased over time. In some cases, both coexist but have certain contextual constraints.

Likewise, irregular plurals from Latin sometimes coexist with regular plurals. Which one is preferred or predictable in any given circumstance is not always clear.

In any case, the matter of spelling here can be a question of what system to assign the word. Once decided, the spelling becomes predictable. It would be inefficient to spell any member of the following set of words from an individual word standpoint.

I.			II.		A marks forms which I have
calf	calv	es			read and/or heard although some
dwarf	dwarv	es-B	dwarf	s	dictionaries do not recognize
elf	elv	es	elf	s-A	their existence, or standard use.
hoof	hoov	es	hoof	s	B marks archaic forms still
knif e	kniv	es	knif	es-A	found in dialect or literary use.
leaf	leav	es	leaf	s-C	Finally, C marks the abbreviated
loaf	loav	es			reference to the plural-form
roof	roov	es-B	roof	s	name of the Canadian hockey
wharf	wharv	es	wharf	s	team: the Toronto Mapleleafs.
wif e	wiv	es			

(Note: classifying v-forms as system I. not II. is relative, not absolute. Sound-it-out works for any form people use themselves. System I. assignment reflects the need for 'elfs' and/or 'knifes' speakers to recall that standard use requires the v-forms in plural.)

	III.	II.
appendix	appendices	appendixes
index	indIces	indexes
codex	codIces	codexes
matrix	matrices	matrixes
thorax	thoraces	thoraxes
vertex	vertIces	vertexes

Capital 'I' marks a vowel as well as consonant change. 'E,' plurals unaccented in system II. have some accentuation in system III. plurals.

Above words except 'thorax' are system III of Latin origin. Contrastively, more common system III. words of Greek origin ending in '-is' lack a system II. plural option. Examples are 'analysis, basis, crisis,' and 'oasis,' whose plurals are 'analyses, bases, crises' and 'oases.

ORIGIN VERSUS PHONOSYMBOLISM: -IZE/-ISE

Vocabulary III. ends four verb sets with the same two sounds-- two of Greek origin, two of Latin origin. American English spells three sets quite regularly. (This section depends largely on Upward 2001.)

1.   Greek-origin verbs: 'ana-lyze, para-lyze, hydr-o-lyze.' Noun forms take 's' in American English: 'ana-lys-is, para-lys-is, hydr-o-lys-is.'
2.   Latin-origin verbs where the sounds are part of a cell. The cell does not stand by itself without an attached prefix.

ad-vise	com-prise	com-pro-mise	circ-um-cise
de-vise	enter-prise	de-mise	ex-cise
im-pro-	sur-prise	sur-mise	
re-vise			de-spise
super-vise			
tele-vise			dis-guise

The group containing 'prise' often winds up misspelled 'prize' e.g. 'surprize' because of misidentification with the latter cell.

3.   Greek-origin words where word without suffix usually stands alone:

"-y" end-ing nouns:		other end-ing nouns:		"-al/-il" end-ing adjectives		excep-tions:	
agon-[y]	-ize	auth-or	-ize	centr-al	-ize	bapt	ize
apo-log-[y]	-ize	char-ac-t-er	-ize	civ-il	-ize	dram-a-t	-ize
col-on-[y]	-ize	com-put-e	-ize	fert-il(e)	-ize	em-phas	-ize
jeo-pard-[y]	-ize	crit-ic	-ize	gen-er-al	-ize	ex-orc	-ize
scrut-in-[y]	-ize	max-im	-ize	cryst-al(l)	-ize	hypn-o-t	-ize
sub-sid-[y]	-ize	mesmer	-ize	in-dustr-i-	-ize	mech-an	-ize
summ-ar-[y]	-ize	org-an	-ize	foss-il	-ize	min-im	-ize
sym-path-[y]	-ize	press-ur(e)	-ize	in-stit-u-t-		mod-er-n	-ize
		publ-ic	-ize	tion-al	-ize		
		re-volu-t-ion	-ize	mater-i-al	-ize		
		sym-bol	-ize	loc-al	-ize		
				ut-il	-ize		
				mob-il(e)	-ize		
				nat-ion-al	-ize		
				nat-ur-al	-ize		
				neut-er-al	-ize		
				pen-al	-ize		
				pol-ar	-ize		
				rat-ion-al	-ize		
				re-al	-ize		
				spec-i-al	-ize		
				vis-u-al	-ize		

4.   The fourth group of verbs has its origin in an -ise suffix of Latin origin. However, since they semantically and phonetically resemble the main '-ize' group, some are more commonly spelled with '-ize.'

ex-erc-ise	merch-and-ise/-ize	re-cogn-ize
franch-ise	ad-vert-ise/-ize	

Is all of this not confusing enough? It gets worse. British usage allows '-ise' to be used in almost all the above cases, while allowing American use, as a variant.

The 's' is then possible and frequent in words like 'organisation.' It is little wonder that quite a few people have trouble choosing the 's' or 'z' in many cases.

WHICH SYSTEM SHOULD BE UNDERSTOOD?

Some unconscious sorting goes on all the time. Whereas some vocabulary is common to many communication situations, other vocabulary is restricted to certain situations or to certain contexts. Naturally, a word may have different meanings in different circumstances.

Multiple spelling systems offer a possibility absent in unitary spelling systems. The same letter string can be pronounced differently depending on how the reader's interpret their system membership. Below identically spelled words have different system-dependent meanings and pronunciations.

I.	'agape'	'bases'	'Wagner'	'dove'	'live'*
			Richard "Composer"	"bird"	verb
II.	"mouth wide open"	"plural of base."	Robert "Actor"	"past tense of dive"	adject-ive
III.	"Christian fellow-ship meal"	"plural of basis"			

The group IV. word 'résumé' spelled without its accents would be a another two-group word partnered with group II. 'resume,' meaning "continue."

The above pronunciations as well as the meanings of the identically spelled words are distinguishable by differences in system membership. Context is the clue allowing readers to narrow the choice between doublets to the suitable options.

Memory of systems rather than memory of words is key. Spelling doublets--with different pronunciations, distinguished by context or meaning alone--must be memorized in system I. Common examples of the latter are:

'bow,'	"posture"	'lead,'	"metal"
	"knot";		"guide"
'row,'	"argument"		
	"line,"	'read,'	"past"
	use oars";		"present"

VARIED COMPLICATIONS

In vocabulary IV.—final letters often do not have English values. Most occur at ends of French loanwords. Below, vocabulary II. and IV. contrast.

II.	IV.
alphabet, asset, blanket,	'ballet, beret, bouquet,
bonnet, budget, bullet,	buffet, cachet, chalet,
poet, faucet, hamlet,	crochet, croquet, filet,
velvet, pellet, outlet.	gourmet, parquet, sachet.'

Some words cannot fall directly into one of the four categories because they are hybrids. Some cells are from one vocabulary while others are from another vocabulary.

Latin-Greek and Greek-Latin hybrids abound, but they are both from vocabulary III. Two-vocabulary hybrids include the examples below.

Greek-English		Latin-English	
tele-cast	noun/verb	in-side	adverb/noun/preposition
anti-knock	adjective	re-fill	noun/verb

My own candidate for worst English spelling is 'four-teen' and 'four' versus 'for-ty.' The cells share both meaning and pronunciation. Thus, the spelling difference violates both system II. and III. rules; neither sound-it-out nor spell-the-cell works. Needing to memorize the difference forces them into system I. vocabulary.

ETYMOLOGY CAN GUIDE, NOT GUARANTEE

The previous analyses and presentations do not always follow etymological dictionaries. This occurs whether words are Latin, Greek or French imports, natives, or Low German or Scandinavian kin.

Most speakers know little or nothing about their own or any other language's history. People make what sense they can out of what they inherit or borrow, making unwitting reassociations and reanalyses. The process is continuous, appearing in constant misspellings, some predictable, and even successful. For example, the word 'whole,' from Anglo-Saxon, relates to 'hale, heal, healthy' and originally meant "complete" in the sense of "sound of body."

The Oxford English Dictionary's 1961 supplement to its 1933 edition listed 'hol-is-t-ic' and 'hol-is-m'—from Greek 'holoc' "whole, entire, complete." These words began to be used in the 20th. century. An occasional misspelling of 'wholism' and 'wholistic' is predictable. Looking at old dictionaries around my house, I found no spelling for 'holistic' or 'holism' in a Webster's Collegiate Dictionary (1936.) However, a Random House College Dictionary (1979), a half century later, listed not only 'holism' and 'holistic,' but also 'wholism' and 'wholistic.'

The latter forms listed 'h-' form counterparts with the usual definitions without any other notation. The 'wh-' forms moved from misspellings to correct spellings in half a century, at least in some circles.

Less clearly related is the spelling 'miniscule' which has replaced 'minuscule' in many venues, including a major newspaper. Cornell Kimball (first entry) devotes a page to the former's social progress from misspelling to variant. Although guides and spell checkers reject it, current editions of major dictionaries and usage books list the variant 'miniscule.'

Citing several sources, Kimball noted that 'miniscule,' appearing in the 1900's, did not become commonly used until the 1940's. 'Miniscule' currently appears three times as much as 'minuscule' in a Boston Globe study.

Historically, 'min-us-c-ule' comes from a Latin comparative of 'min-or,' namely 'min-us.' When the suffixes '–c-ul' are added to certain Latin words, they often make the word mean something smaller. So 'miniscule' might be phrased "more minor" or "very small."

Pronunciation of the second vowel may play a role in some dialects. However, it is also possible that 'min-I-' has a clearer connection in many speakers' consciousness to "very small" than 'min-us-' does.

Interestingly enough, the misspelling/variant spelling remains in system three. Except possibly for the 's,' 'min-I-s-c-ule' remains composed of Latin word cells.

Some misspellings, not always predictable, make sense after the fact. In an advanced writing class which I teach, 'on sight' sometimes replaces 'on site' inspection.

In a biblical and classical literature course which I also teach, 'last rights' occasionally spells 'last rites.' I suspect this is especially American, i.e. one's last 'entitlement' from one's denomination.

A Communications' Department colleague, Dr. Kerran Sanger, reports 'periarticles' for 'periodicals' and an intriguing 'higherarchy' for 'hierarchy.' An English Department colleague, Professor Patricia McNaney, reports reading 'pedastool' for 'pedestal' in a freshman composition.

These 'misspellings' still yield to a spell-the-cell division even though they are "wrong" and sometimes hybrid. The misspellings in the first line below remain in three system III. just as the correct spellings in the second line.

| peri-art-ic-le=s | high-er-arch-y | ped-a-stool |
| peri-od-ic-al=s | hier -arch-y | ped-e-st -al |

Misspellings and mispronunciations, necessarily considered "mistakes" for legitimate social and economic goals of education, often reveal unconscious reanalyses, differing from the conventional. I believe that the "misspellings" above are examples of potential restructurings.

The replacement cells in the above examples are generally cells of greater frequency. 'High' is a word and cell of high frequency. Conversely, 'hier-o-glyph-ic' and 'hier-o-phant' are not part of everyone's everyday vocabulary.

These respellings differ from simple homonym/homophone errors like to/two/too or its/it's. For one thing, they are the same parts of speech, nouns as indicated by paradigmatic or other suffixes. For another, the misspellings make some sense in the way that they have been respelled.

The misspellings discussed above come close to that class of mistakes called malapropisms which are often produced by less educated speakers. A malapropism sounds much like the form that should be used. Consequently, most teachers can figure out what a pupil or student intended to say.

Malapropisms reveal an inappropriate restructuring, but sometimes the malapropism replaces its original. 'A-prop-os' is from system IV. and commonly means "pertinent" or "opportune." 'Ap-prop-i-ate' is from vocabulary III. and commonly means "suitable" or "proper."

The difference in meaning is slight, and the first two syllables share consonant sounds and vowel spellings. Now common are sentences like 'That comment is very apropos.' with 'apropos' used merely as an upscale alternative to 'appropriate.'

Paul Brians' (2000) website, "Common Errors in English," attests the widespread use of this association by its very inclusion on his site.

Brians reminds his readers that the meaning of 'Apropos' is "relevant, connected with what has gone before." It is not an all-purpose substitute for 'appropriate.'

'Abrogate' and 'abdicate' may illustrate a similar case of an increasingly sanctioned malapropism. Both words come from vocabulary III. with 'abrogate' commonly meaning to "repeal, annul, or cancel". 'Abdicate' commonly meant to "surrender an office, trust or dignity."
    Again, the difference in meaning is slight. The accent, prefixes, and suffixes are the same: 'AB-rog-Ate, AB-dic-Ate.' When I was decades younger, I heard people complaining about those 'abrogating' responsibilities. Currently, from all sides, I hear the same complaints about those who are 'abdicating' responsibilities.
    Sometimes, it is difficult to determine which word is the malapropism, and which is to be considered the original/correct word. William Safire (2000, pp. B-27 & B-28.) discusses words of different origin which modify 'face' in the expressions: 'barefaced/baldfaced/boldfaced lie.'
    Safire related that in 1590, Shakespeare introduced the term 'bare-faced' in Midsummer Night's Dream, and it meant "whiskerless." By 1760, in Lawrence Sterne's Tristam Shandy, it meant "shameless." In 1591, Shakespeare introduces 'boldfaced' which meant "confident" and soon after, "impudent."
    In the 1600's through 1800's, 'bald' meant "white"; therefore, 'bald-face' would mean "white-faced." Safire does not mention it, but I am speculating that, once it meant "hairless," its development paralleled 'bare faced.' Consequently, any of the three alternatives now means something like "audacious" before 'lie.'
    I am not sure that even knowledgeable people cannot have a conscious and subconscious structure difference simultaneously. A personal example would be the word: 'dys-funct-ion.'
    I know that the prefix, 'dys-' is from Greek and means "ill" or "bad," and 'dys-funct-ion' from this perspective means "bad function." However, "not function" closely resembles that, and the Latin prefix 'dis-' which means "apart, away" or "not" would serve just as well. Additionally, it sounds the same and occurs more frequently.
    As a pupil, I originally misspelled this word as 'disfunction' and am sure that others still do. I suspect that my subconscious has 'dis-' and that the spelling 'dys-' is (or was) memorized as an anomalous spelling. That is, it is like anyone's learning to spell 'pro-ceed, ex-ceed, suc-ceed' where 'pro-cede, ex-cede, suc-cede' are expected.

I was both raised in and live in a northern dialect area. Words like 'Sunday,' 'tomorrow' and 'Mississippi' can have long vowels under weak stress, particularly in final syllables.

Unstressed front syllables like those in 'receive' and 'demote' vary between long and typical unstressed vowels. I do not know, but can only speculate about, what conditioning factors favor one pronunciation rather than another.

In any case, the first syllable of the word 'rapport,' can sometimes be pronounced with a long vowel in this speech area. When it does, it is usually pronounced as if it were spelled with an 'e', not an 'a' i.e. like 'repour.'

Rarely, the word is spelled 'report' or 'repore.' I believe the common pronunciation and the rare spelling reflect an unconscious reassignment of the uncommon 'ra-' to the more common 're-.'

The absence of the written 't' in the pronunciation signals a system III. vocabulary item. Thus, an "atypical" spelling, within a French, not English, origin, item does not present a major spelling problem to most. (The double 'p' simply marks the short vowel.)

A complete discussion should not ignore the fact that the word historically had its origin in French 're-ap-port-er.' In its modern English meaning, "sympathetic relation or connection," there is no particular reference to "back" or "again." Thus, the three shared conditions: "consonant 'r'," "unstressed vowel," and "initial position" probably account for the pronunciation and spelling mentioned.

GRAMMAR AND USAGE IMPACTING SPELLING

The following material is not immediately recognizable as relating to spelling and phonosymbolism. However, there are a variety of restructurings beyond reanalyzing a word from one system to another. Sometimes the reanalysis of cells leads to a reanalysis of the function of the cells. This, in turn, can affect the spelling.

First, alternative grammar rules interfere with learning standard-usage rules, especially word choice. For example, the English pattern for monosyllabic descriptive adjectives likely fosters nonstandard 'He did good.' over 'He did well.'

Descriptive adverb counterparts are usually identical or add '-ly.': beautiful, beautifully; nice, nicely etc. Perhaps, 'goodly' with a different meaning and adjective use helped let an atypical form 'well' become the standard adverb counterpart to 'good.'

Ordinary speech often has 'Who did you say?' and 'It's me.' not 'Whom did you say?' and 'It is I.' The former are deemed colloquial (standard but informal variants) of the latter.

Later Modern English uses more word order and less inflection than earlier Modern English. Imagine a contemporary toy store named "Toys Я We." The standard choices, once native for some, are now new options to consciously memorize rather than unconscious grammar output.

Modern American English personal-pronoun case selection differs "colloquially." Generally, subject case occurs before a verb and object case after, whether the pronoun is respectively a subject or object, or not. There are special additional rules for pronouns in a compound or series; particularly complex is the pronoun alternation between I and me.

In formal venues, many say 'Let's keep this between you and I' more often than "me." This is odd not as it is nonstandard, but as informality usually favors ,e.g., 'me, her. us' where standard usage has 'I, she, we.' Hoffman (1989) and Parker et al. (1988) address some of these concerns.

Such problems are more subtle than more obvious conflicts from foreign languages or from nonstandard American vernaculars. Familiar examples of the latter are Ebonics/African American Vernacular English, Appalachian/Southern Mountain English, Hawaian Pidgin/Creole, and Louisiana Creole.

A standard vs. vernacular problem which teachers and others note is absent/incorrect plural, possessive, and third singular suffixes. Often deemed misspellings, they result instead from standard and vernacular grammar interference. Examples include 'He start today;' and 'She work hard.'

The absence of the 's' can be called a spelling error. However, the cause is a difference in grammar between Standard American English and African-American Vernacular English. Similar, but not identical, differences can be found between Standard British English and some rural dialects in Southern English. These too result from interference between the standard and dialect grammars.

Such loss of inflections is not limited to dialect interference as a cause. Conflict between or among languages can produce similar symptoms. Some Asian writers of English produce forms lacking the tense and plural suffixes because the grammar of their languages/ varieties does not require them.

Dialect/language differences, not inattention, inability, or mental, social or physical problems, can cause "errors" persisting among many for generations. If used across the country, they are national. If only in a region or among specific groups, errors are dialectal (unless an identifiable second language is involved.)

Spelling correctly requires mapping spellings to standard English productions after vernacular to standard translations occur. Some learn this themselves out of awareness; others can be taught before the writing stage. Most others, if they manage at all, adjust while editing their writing. Not all mismatches are between nonstandard and standard grammars. Some are between informal and formal standard English grammar, which interference may cause "nonstandard" spellings.

"CORRECTLY" SPELLING GRAMMTICAL FORMS MAY VIOLATE STANDARD SPELLING

As mentioned earlier, people constantly reanalyze and reassociate causing new spellings for such reanalyzed and reassociated words. What follows are candidates for common misspellings from mismatches between people's actual grammar and standard English grammar".

'Alright' is a nonstandard or, at best, non-preferred alternative to standard: 'all right.' Some references hint that 'alright' may result from 'analogy' with words like 'already' and 'altogether.' The 'all,' now perceived as prefix 'al-,' makes adverbs from other speech parts, e.g., 'always' and 'also.'

The historical adverb versus adjective/adverb combination 'all right' has become the adverb 'alright.' My idiolect has both 'alright' and 'all right' in - syntactic contrast. Yet, I spell both in the latter manner to maintain prescriptive "standards."

The former an adverb, depending on context, means "excellent, fitting, acceptable, tolerable, permissible." The latter, two words, has an adverb (a.k.a. 'qualifier, specifier') which modifies the adjective/ adverb 'right.' The meaning is fairly limited: "correct in every element, member or detail."

A parallel pair--where both are standard--are 'already' and 'all ready.' 'Aready' is an adverb and means "previously", or when surprised, "so soon?" In contrast, 'all ready' means "totally ready" or "prepared."

Such word-cell function shifts are common. The words 'full' and 'less'—besides remaining adjectives themselves—also became adjective suffixes, spelled respectively: '-ful' and '-less.' The first suffix has a changed spelling and the second, a changed meaning ('without'); compare 'help less' and 'helpless.'

In any case, a cell once functioning as an independent word may become a suffix in some contexts. This sometimes results in a spelling change. The prefix 'a-' marks adverbs, (some adjectives and prepositions) and has different historical origins, usually Anglo-Saxon prepositions or Latin prefixes.

These forms were generally vowel plus consonant with the prefix consonant lost before the consonants of words prefixed. Examples below are mostly prefixed historically with the 'an' spelling of the preposition 'on.'

a_-bove	a_-foot	a_-gain	a_-head	a_-new	a_-part	a_-round	a_-sea etc.
on	on	on	on	of	ad-	on	on

Historically and currently, 'a lot' meaning "a large amount" is clearly "indefinite article plus noun." The plural noun without an article unambiguously reflects its noun structure in 'Lots of them are needed.'

However, in a context where the meaning is "often," the grammar may be different: 'We saw them a lot.' In this case, a common misspelling closes the space: 'It happened alot.'

Possibly, misspellers' colloquial grammar no longer has "article plus noun," but "adverb-prefix plus noun." If so, the "misspelling" reflects a new--though unsanctioned and unrecognized--adverb.

In such a case, the misspelling would not be a problem of mapping sound to symbol. The sound to symbol match is not bad. Nor would the misspelling (the loss of space between the words) be the re=sult of inattention or poor memory. Rather, it would reflect the "true" word-cell spelling of the speaker who writes it although it is currently rated nonstandard.

A Western New York local grammatical use different from formal textbook grammar causes a "punctuation" problem. The word 'although' with lower rather than high stress on the second syllable is the same as in any other English dialect. It is what school grammars term "subordinate conjunction, subordinator" etc.

It can also occur under strong stress and is often punctuated thus: 'He did it; although, he was not sure about it.' In this latter case, "although" appears to function much like a conjunctive adverb such as 'however.'

As a writing teacher, I must correct people who punctuate 'although' as they punctuate 'however' and 'therefore.' Consequently, I have to correct people who punctuate 'although' properly (for their dialect.)

That creates something of a pedagogical paradox. The linguist in me is in conflict with the English composition teacher.

In the latter role, I must facilitate standard usage to support my students future credibility in the work place. To accomplish this, I sometimes (as shown above) must instruct people to punctuate a word incorrectly for their local dialect.

CONCLUSION

Sometimes, the precise mechanism of a restructuring is not absolutely clear. Sound resemblance, frequency, familiarity, contextual associations etc. may all play roles.

Two examples of the not-quite-clear, not-quite-mysterious restructurings are 'nucular' and 'momento.' These seem, on the surface, to be simple lapses, but I hear and read them quite often.

The correct spelling 'nuc-l-e-ar' rather than 'nuc-ul-ar' should be easily abstractable from 'nuc-l-e-us.' Is it the influence of the preceding 'u' or the great frequency of '-ul' in scientific words which affects the spelling? Is it a combination of both?

Likewise, the correct spelling 'memento' rather than 'momento' should easily be determined from 'mem-or-i-al,' 'mem-oir,' 'mem-or-and-um,' 'mem-or-ab-le,' 'mem-or-ab-il-i-a.' etc.
Yet, so many people make the error; the reason is not clear. Does the final 'o' of memento affect the misspelling, or do the following 'o's' in the five examples affect the choice? Is some association like "remember the moment" involved or does the misspelling result from some combination of all or any of them?

It would be a mistake to assume that all misspellings from word-cell confusion is in system III. Such situations also exist in systems I. and II. There are notable cases where both sound symbolism and formal/informal grammar differences make both choice and spelling of variants difficult.

Warriners' (1986, p. 189) lists three pairs of verbs which he considers especially problematic. He considers them more difficult to use correctly than other verbs.

Consequently, they require more study and practice than other verbs. His list is 'lie, lay; sit, set; lie, lay." Warriner considers the last pair to be the most difficult.

In various textbooks, these verbs join others like 'hang, hung, hung; hang, hanged, hanged.' English handbook fare for generations, they will likely remain so. Why are such pairs so problemsome?

'sit,	sat,	sat;	set,	set	set'
'lay,	lai=d,	lai=d;	lie,	lay,	lai=n'
'raise,	rais=ed,	rais=ed;	rise,	rose,	ris=en'
'hang,.	hang=ed	hang=ed;	hang,	hung,	hung'
'fell,	fell=ed,	fell=ed;	fall,	fell,	fall=en'

There are four good reasons why people confuse them:

1. Pairs that are confused all have the same consonants in their roots.
2. Though meanings differ, they are related, some pairs more than others.
3. Informal may differ from formal use, and standard from nonstandard. Complications arise in the use of terms like 'lie' and 'lay' in relation to erotic activity.
4. Distinctions such as irregular and regular as well as transitive and intransitive are subtle and easily forgotten terms and concepts. People may use such distinctions for discussion, description and analysis, but certainly do not use them in unconscious speech acts.

Standard use requires 'hanged' for people and 'hung' for pictures. Yet, I have never heard actors in a western lynch-mob scene who had not demanded that the alleged perpetrator be "hung."

Some pair problems are more dialect-specific than others. The 'lie' and 'lay' problem seems more general than any of the others.

CORE AND PERIPHERY

A number of distinctions formed the earlier discussion. These include distinctions among the four vocabularies and among the types of problems that occur as well as their interactions. A final distinction is necessary.

The four systems give speakers several possible choices, depending on where sound and sense resemblances lead. However, the four systems are not rigidly bounded.

Words in a system's core have all or most of the characteristics described for the figure earlier . More peripheral words like system III."s "native" may yield to system II's sound-it-out strategy 'na + tive.' This assumes a link made with 'I' to '-ive' rather than 'ave, eve,' or 'ove.' In comparison, sounding-out the second syllable of 'con + science' is difficult, if not impossible. This makes it, more centrally, system III.: 'con-sci-en-ce.'

Earlier, I put 'rhyme' within system II., but some may memorize the silent 'h' and the 'y" for 'i.' For them, at least, it would be in system I.'s memorization vocabulary.

English spelling, an unconscious fourfold sorting system, comes from generations of speakers and writers, interpreting borrowings from sources, usually outside their awareness. (Coined scientific terms entering vocabulary III. are a notable exception.)

Some borrowings are so substantial that spelling rules of the borrowed writing systems stay fully or partially preserved. Conflicts among the four systems have caused some reanalyzes and respellings different from any in the donor languages' writing systems.

Westcott (1979, p. 82) distinguished spellings which reflect their historical origins from reshaped spellings which do not reflect their historical origins. He called traditional etymology: "lineal etymology" and the less systematic reshapings: "collateral etymology."

Tyma (1979, p. 53) made a similar distinction between spellings which do and do not reflect their historical origins. He called the former spellings examples of "vertical" and the latter spellings examples of "horizontal" etymology.

PICKING STRATEGIES

That the above strategies are possible does not mean that spellers routinely use them. Many students rely on memorization, sound-it-out, and p.c. spell checkers.

Sadly, the same ironic paradox applies to spell checkers as to dictionaries. "They help better more than poor spellers." Poor spellers' dilemma is that spell-checkers do not flag poor homonym choices.

Most spellers likely memorize many French and Latinate borrowings, unaware of the former's half sound-out, half memorize strategy. Some may have had Latin and Greek word-cell exposure, but the spell-the-cell strategy is likely unknown, at least consciously.

When my children were younger, I watched some science-fiction based children's cartoons and action adventures, to monitor violence. It seemed that system III. cells occurred without specific meaning, for high-tech. ambiance.

I did not systematically study these programs. My impression, however, was that they often used system III. cells in names for villains and sometimes heroes. If robots were enemies, system III. cells were more equally frequent on both sides.

I have read that boys watch such shows more than girls. Do boys have a larger unconscious inventory of system III. word cells? If so, this exposure does not seem to have helped boys spell or read any better than girls.

There are senior citizens of my acquaintance who have had no scientific interest or training. Yet, some have taught themselves to recognize organic chemical names for active ingredients of various over-the-counter drugs.

This is done to save money by identifying and purchasing generic counterparts to brand-name drugs. (Pharmacies facilitate this by inviting consumers to compare active ingredients in cheaper store labels to those in more expensive name brands.)

System III. cells are found in books at different levels as vocabulary and spelling aids. Some even make elementary cell divisions and discuss ori-gins. Warriner's secondary grammar and composition text's treatment (1982, pp. 632-647/1986, pp. 900-915.) was excellent, but too short to be effective.

Mastering Latin and Greek word-cell spelling regularity is not a curriculum standard. Without it, memorization strategies are taxed with strings like: 'anti-dis-e-stab-l-ish-ment-ar-i-an-is-m,' though one might get close with sound-it-out.

PERSONALS EXAMPLES OF WRESTLING WITH SPELL-THE-CELL

The educational system has contributed to solving word-cell problems—despite often unsystematic applications. I gained from such instruction as a child and youth. The following relates situations in which I encountered solutions to spelling problems with "word-cell" oriented approaches

The dialect that I spoke did not distinguish certain prefixes, by pronunciation when the cells were unaccented. That is, I could spell 'inTER-rog-ate, PRE-ci-ous, PRE-face, PRO-cess' and 'PRO-ject' by the sounding-out strategy. However, until I saw the following sets in written form, I had no idea that the unaccented prefixes were distinct.

inter-change	intra-mur-al	Some sort of spelling book distin-
inter-nat-ion-al	intra-state	guished such words by meaning not
inter-med-i-ate		pronunciation. I had perceived all of
inter-miss-ion	intro-duce	these as 'inter-.'

Pronunciation rules would not have helped me to distinguish what I had pronounced the same. The existence of the treatment alerted me, even at that early age, that I was not the only English speaker with such a spelling problem. Others shared the problem of spelling large sets of words other than how they actually pronounced them.

Doing well in English literature and/or writing classes was always a high personal priority. Therefore, I put considerable effort into correcting my misspellings, not just for the short, but for the long run.

I linked 'introduce' to the abbreviated 'intro.' 'Inter-' as "between" and 'intra-' as "inside" worked well. The next set did not work as well.

per-ceive	pre-cede	pro-ced-ure
per-cent	pre-dict	pro-cess-ion
per-form	pre-fer	pro-duct-ion
per-fume	pre-tend	pro-fess-or
(To this group, I might add the native Anglo-Saxon word 'pretty.')	part-ic-ul-ar (Historical)	par-t-ic-ul-ar (Perceptual?

I had perceived all of these as beginning with 'per.' Some spelling books also distinguished these, but it was not as helpful as with the previous set. 'Per-': "through," "thorough," or "very"; 'pre-': "before (time)," and 'pro-': "in favor of" or "before (time or space)" were harder to apply. I did not know what many cells following the prefixes meant, and either 'pre-' or 'pro-' could reflect the referent: "before."

I eventually sorted them out by two techniques. One was listening to people who distinguished them. Once I saw different spellings, I guessed that others probably pronounced the respective prefixes differently.

I was right, and I listened and imitated them. Their oral productions, though different from mine, nonetheless, were easier to remember than the written form.

Another technique which I used was linking related accented and unaccented cells once I saw them written and could recognize shared meanings. For example, 'per-cess-ion' became 'pro-cess-ion' when I could link the latter to 'PRO-cess.' Likewise, 'per-fer' could become 'pre-fer' after linking the latter to 'PRE-fer-en-ce.'

'Particular' and longer words incorporating unstressed 'part-' was a simple matter of memorization. Much later, I recognized the connection to 'part' and 'PART-ic-le.'

Hearing the form 'pre-vert' for 'per-vert' makes me wonder whether there are speakers who have 'pre-' where I had 'per-'. That is, do some speakers have 'pre-' for both 'pre-' and 'per-'? I doubt it, and suspect overcorrection.

That is, after being corrected for 'per-fer, per-cede, per-dict,' some people probably induce a rule: "in formal situations, change 'per-' to 'pre'." Naturally, the rule would work for genuine 'pre-' cases, but would create overcorrections like 'pre-vert' with conventional 'per-' prefixes.

Additionally, I had merged 'hyper-' and 'hypo-,' with or without final 'r.' Contrasting "over" and "under" was futile since I used both in very few words.

Memorizing served for 'hyper-act-ive, hyper-son-ic,' and 'hypo-derm-ic, hypo-chondr-i-ac' etc. "Under" would not have helped me with the last because I would have had no clue what '-chondr-i-ac' might have meant.

I noticed such things, aware that many classmates had not, which likely figured in my later becoming a linguist. What had bene-fited me had not helped many peers without an encompassing scheme for teachers and students to use. Smith and Sustakoski have provided a basis for such a scheme.

Multiple systems help to look at old arguments from a new perspective. One example is the ceaseless argument between those for and against teaching Latin and Greek cells for spelling and vocabulary improvement. The "pro" group show how learning common etymology links the cells.

Learning the links and spelling of cells helps students learn how to spell and use many more words which contain those cells. This includes words which they have not yet encountered.

The "anti" group shows how often the etymologies are false and how links among historically related cells are often less than perfect. Words of non-Latin and Greek origin which wind up resem-bling them for all practical purposes are discounted in such denun-ciations.

The four-system approach does not see the two positions as necessarily exclusive. If people have taken non system-III. words and reanalyzed and respelled them as system III. words, so be it. We cer-tainly have to spell words where they are, not where they were.

Why ignore system III. strategies for words with non-histo-rical Latin and Greek cells? So what, if such cells have not actually come from Latin and Greek?

Native or naturalized, system III. is system III. As the folk saying goes: 'If it acts like a duck, and quacks like a duck, it's a duck.' Since elementary and secondary education may treat System III. word cells unsystematically, many people lack either conscious or uncon-scious spell-the-cell mastery. However, not all areas of education can afford such neglect. Health, life and physical science practitioners have no option but to learn whatever system III. vocabulary is necessary for their respective disciplines.

SPELL-THE-CELL IN THE SERVICE OF SCIENCE

The health, life and physical sciences employ a strategy, re-quiring even more than spell-the-cell. Users must not only spell-the-cell, but also memorize fixed Latin and Greek cell meanings used in their respective disciplines.

In the libraries and book stores of health science campuses, text after text teaches the cells used for the discipline. Some cells form very necessary technical terms which ordinary language does not pro-vide. Other terms are jargon masquerading as technical terms al-hough they have excellent equivalents in ordinary language.

There is a long history of using Latin and Greek cells in scien-tific terminology. After the Western Roman Empire fell, Latin continu-ed as the language of the Church.

From medieval times, it was also the language of University instruction in Law, Medicine and Theology. Directly borrowing Greek and Latin cells to name instruments may have begun with the naming of Galileo's "telescope." (Boorstin, p. 322)

Classification in Zoology and Botany (Boorstin, pp. 420-446) followed a similar route with the works of Ray and Linnaeus. They worked during the period of the French, American and Industrial revo-lutions.

Consequently, shared technical Latin- and Greek-origin voca-bulary has been created from the Roman Empire's height until the pre-sent. Most such choices have been pragmatically-based reflexes from this long-standing tradition in Western sciences of borrowing classical cells. Other terms are somewhat suspect.

Why did Freud's German 'es,' 'ich,' and 'über-ich' become Latin 'id,' 'ego,' and 'super-ego' in English psychological terminology? A direct English translation would be "it," "I," and "super/over-I." The latter would be simpler and easier to understand but definitely lack social-science cachet.

Whether genuine or argot, system-III. terms have a number of uses beyond professional discussions. Such terms identify fellow health professionals to one another.

They promote professional solidarity, and they provide material for practioners to translate to their patients as part of their professional services. A fairly limited number of cells make up most long scientific words.

Sometimes, scientifically-employed cells closely mirror original meanings, as in anatomy. In other cases, like chemistry, word-cell meanings have been specialized and frozen, and may not directly reflect original meanings. Below are samples of systematic technical use of System III. cells.

The examples below are just a small sample of what is used and what occurs. The choice of word cells represented do not reflect the full range of possible variation. However, these examples should suffice to illustrate the important role of system III. vocabulary in both natural and life sciences.

MEDICINE		ANATOMY/MEDICINE-	
==it-is	inflam-mation,	derm==/ derm-a(t))==-	skin,
==om-a	tumor,	gastr==	stomach,
==os-is	abnormal state,	card-i==	heart,
==ed-em-a	swelling,	carp==	wrist,
==seps-is	infection.	rhin==	nose.

Before many vowels, the rightmost list adds the linking vowel "-o-".

INORGANIC CHEMISTRY		ORGANIC CHEMISTRY	
==ate	salt of acid ending in -ic,	==ase	enzyme,
		==ol	alcohol,
==ite	salt of acid- ending in -ous	==ose	sugars, some carbo-
==I-um	name of an element.		hyrdrates, & some protein derivatives.

Above, strings rather than single cells are often glossed in these disciplines. Equal signs, before or after, indicate such strings, with hyphens marking cell boundaries within them. Glosses are from dictionaries and classically-based vocabulary aids in this work's bibliography.

Clustering words sharing sound and/or spelling and/or grammatical function has always been part of spelling and vocabulary building. Examples are clusters like 'could, should, would;' 'bought, fought, sought, thought, wrought; caught, taught' etc.

FINAL REMARKS

'Vocabulary' and 'system,' nearly interchangeable in the above discussion, are not identical. 'Vocabulary' is a word list associated by two factors. Its inventory shares a an overall spelling strategy, and a plurality/majority of its listings share historical origins.

'System' includes the above features plus two more. One is additional sub-rules in a vocabulary which insure correct spellings. For example, "silent e" and "double consonants" mark long and short vowels in system II.

Another is a vocabulary's characteristic sound-letter mappings. Examples are 'ph' for f-sounds and 'ch' for k-sounds in system III's Greek sub-vocabulary.

Some system II. rules are so powerful that they transcend a vocabulary's limits, to affect others as well. The best example is (c=s) before 'I, e' and 'y' and (c=k) before consonants, and 'a, o' and 'u.'

Thus, 'k' usually represents k-sounds before 'e, I' and 'y' in the first three vocabularies. As noted before, 'k' in 'kitten' has an obscured relation to 'cat.' Likewise 'k' in 'in-voke, convoke, revoke, provoke' etc. masks their relations to 'invocation, convocation, revocation, provocation' et al.

Now, with four systems of vocabulary identified, more associations of spellings--within a single vocabulary, employing a common strategy--are possible. Also, matching the most efficient strategy to the appropriate vocabulary can be implemented with more confidence.

I have synthesized Smith and Sustakoski's insights on English spelling with insights of phonosymbolism from Tyma, Westcott and others. May this synthesis serve as a basis to encourage new and improved spelling lessons and spelling-lesson materials.

BIBLIOGRAPHY

PRINT REFERENCES:

Bloomfield, Leonard. 1933. *Language.* NY: Henry Holt & Co. [pp.240-246.]

Boorstin, Daniel J. 1985. *The Discoverers.* NY: Vintage Books/Random House.

Buriss, Eli E. & Casson, Lionel. 1949. Latin and Greek in Current Use. 2nd. Ed. New York: Prentice-Hall Inc.

Buyers, Sue. 1977, August 20). "English: It's a Foreign Language to many American, Kids." *Buffalo Evening News*, A-8.

Danner, Horace G. 1985. *An Introduction to an Academic Vocabulary, Word Clusters from Latin, Greek and German: a Vade Mecum for the Serious Student.* Lanham, Maryland: U. Press of America. (UPA)

Ehrlich, Ida. 1968. *Instant Vocabulary.* New York: Pocket Books.

Giangrande, Lawrence. 1987, *Latin in the Service of English.* UPA.

Hill, Archibald A. 1958. *Introduction to Linguistic Structures.* New York: Harcourt, Brace & World Inc. [pp. 145-152 and 370-389.]

Hockett, Charles F. 1947. "Problems of Morphemic Analysis." *Language.* 23,321-43.

Hoffman, Melvin J. 1987. "An Aspectual Examination of some Relic English Paradigms." *Proceedings of the 16th. Spring Conference.* Ed. J. Hesch. Buffalo, N.Y.: Niagara Linguistic Society.

_____. 1989. "Who? Me? Or, Accord on Concord Discord." NLS News. (Spring): 5-7 [Feature]

_____. 1990. "Reshuffling of 'Relic' English Paradigms through Phonosymbolism." The *16th. LACUS Forum 1989.* Linguistic Association of Canada and the U.S. (LACUS) Ed. M. Jordan. Columbia, S.C.: Hornbeam Press Inc. (Hornbeam.)

_____. 1982. "Sound Change Versus Social Shibboleths." *The 8th LACUS. Forum 1981.* Eds. W. Gutwinski and G. Jolly. Hornbeam

Laurita, Raymond E. 1991. *Spelling Keys to One Thousand One Words from Ten Greek Based Roots.* Paperback. Camden, ME: Leonardo Press

_____. 1991. Spelling Keys to One Thousand Words from Ten Latin Based Roots. Paperback. Camden, ME: Leonardo Press.

Leuschnig, C. A. E. with Leuschnig, L. J. 1982. Etyma: An Introduction to Vocabulary-Building from Latin and Greek. UPA.

Malkiel, Yakov. 1978. "From Phonosymbolism to Morphosymbolism." in Paradis.

Markel, Norman N. and Hamp, Eric P. 1961. "Connotative Meanings of Certain Phoneme Sequences." Studies in Linguistics, 15, 47-61.

McNaney, Patricia. 1998. Private Communication.

Norback, Craig and Norback, Peter. 1979. The Must Words: the 6000 Most Important Words for a Successful and Profitable Vocabulary. New York: McGraw-Hill Paperback.

Oxford English Dictionary. 1961. 13 vols. London: Oxford U. Press.

Paradis, Michel. Ed. 1978. 4th LACUS Forum 1977. Hornbeam.

Parker, Frank; Riley, Kathryn and Meyer, Charles. 1988. "Case Assignment and the Ordering of Constituents in Coordinate Constructions." American Speech. (Fall): 214-233.

The Random House College Dictionary. 1979. Rev. Ed. by Jess Stein. New York: Random House.

Ramsden, Melvyn. 1993. Rescuing Spelling. Crediton, Devon UK: Southgate Publishers.

Reich, Peter. Ed. 1976. 2nd. LACUS Forum 1975. Hornbeam.

Safire, William. 2000. The New York Times Magazine. (Nov. 5): B-28 & B-29.

Sanger, Kerran. 1998. Private Communication.

Skeat, Walter W. 1963. A Concise Etymological Dictionary of the English Language. New York: Capricorn Books.

Smith, Henry Lee Jr. and Sustakoski, Henry J. 1964 & 1965. "Pronunciation and Spelling " (ch. 8, v. 2.) A Linguistic Approach to English. (2 vv. Rev. ed.). Off. of Ed. Dept. of HEW & SUNY at Buffalo Dept. of Anthropology & Linguistics. (Report No.1856). (ERIC Documentation Service Nos. EDO 21214 & EDO21215.)

Trager, George L. Language and Languages. San Francisco/Scranton: Chandler Publishing Co., 1972

Tyma, Stephen. 1978. "Relation, Synchrony and Diachrony the Analysis and Description of Language." in Paradis.

_____. 1979. "Phonosymbolism, Morphosymbolism and Lexicosmantic Constants." in Wölck and Garvin.

vos Savant, Marilyn. 2000. The Art of Spelling: The Madness and the Method. New York: W. W. Norton.

_____. 2000. "You can Be a Better Speller." Parade Magazine. (August 13): 4-5

Warriner, John. Warriner's English Grammar and Composition: Complete Course.Franklin/Liberty Editions. New York: Harcourt, Brace, Jovanovich, Publishers, 1982/1986.

Webster's Collegiate Dictionary. 1943. 5th. Ed. Springfield, Massachusetts:G.C. Merriam Co.

Westcott, Roger S. 1976. "Allolinguistics: Exploring the Peripheries of Speech." in Reich.

———. 1979. "Lexical Polygenesis: Words as Resultants of Multiple Linguistic Pressures." in Wölck and Garvin.

———. 1980. *Sound and Sense: Linguistic Essays on Phonosemic Subjects.* No. 8. Edward Sapir Monograph Series. Jupiter Press. [Includes two above articles in section: "The scope of language."]

Wölck, Wolfgang and Garvin, Paul L. Eds. 1979. *5th. LACUS Forum 1978.* Hornbeam.

CYBERSOURCES (Accessible as of MAY 2003):

Ager, Simon. "Inuktitut Syllabary." in "Omniglot: A Guide to Writing Systems." 1998-2002--<http://www.omniglot.com/writing/inuktitut.htm>

Ager, Simon. "Serbian and Croatian." in "Omniglot: A Guide to Writing Systems." 1998-2002--<http://www.omniglot.com/writing/serbo-croat.htm>

Bett, Steve. English Spelling Reform Link Page. 1998 <http://victorian.fortunecity.com vangogh/555/Spell/sitemap-l.html>

Branner, David Prager. May 1994, Week 4. Summary: Klang Association. LINGUISTList 5.590. Sat. May 19--<http://www.linguistlist.org/issues/5/5-590.html>

Brians, Paul. Common Errors in English. Revised August 8, 2000-- http://www.wsu.edu/~brians/errors/errors.html>

Brown, A. R. 1998. Spelling Reform in Context: A Typology, List & Bibliography of English Spelling Reform Proposals. 3rd. Ed. Rev. by Christopher Upward. Simplified Spelling Society. October--<http:// www.spellingsociety.org/pubs/pamflets/13-typology.shtml>

The Cherokee Companion. 1997-2000. Profit Systems Software--<http://www. intertribal.net/NAT/Cherokee/WebPgCC1/Cc1home.htm>

Daniel, Aharon. 1999-2000. Official language [India]--<http://adaniel.tripod.com/Languages2.htm>

Eisenberg, J. David. 2000. An Introduction to Korean--<http://www.langintro.com/kintro/>

Gaskell, Gareth. Summary: Phonological Clusters Words. August 1998, Week 3. LINGUIST List 9.1171. Fri. Aug. 21--<http://www.linguistlist.org/issues/9/9-1171.html">

Grossen, Bonita (University of Oregon.) 1997. "A Synthesis of Research on Reading from the National Institute of Child Health and Human Development." The NICHD Research Centers Bibliography. November--<http://www.nrrf.org/synthesis_research.htm>

Hindustani."Encyclopedia.com 2002.--<http://www.encyclopedia.com/html/h/hindustani.asp">

Hiskes, Dolores. 1998. "Explicit or Implicit Phonics: 'Therein Lies the Rub'." from *The Right to Read Report.* February--<http://nrrf.org/essay_Explicit_or_Implicit_Phonics.html">

Holdren, John. Director of Research and Communications, Core Knowledge Foundation. 1995. Not "either/or" but "both/and": Phonics and Whole Language. *Common Knowledge* 8.3 (Summer.)--<http://www.coreknowledge.org/ckproto2about/nwsltr/PhonicsNwsltr.htm>

The Inuktitut language of Tununiq. Travel and Adventure, 1998--<http://www.tununiq.com/masters/iinuk.htm>

Introduction To Korean. No Date--<http://www.tongil.org/ucbooks/kintro//toc.htm>

Ivey, Keith C. (1998) *Beyond Gutenberg.* EEI Press.--<http://web.archive.org./web/20000821084017/http://www.eeicommunications.com/eye/utw/96apr.html>

Juel, Connie. 1994. "Teaching Phonics in the Context of the Integrated Language Arts." *Integrated Language Arts*, ed. L. M. Morrow et al. Needham Heights, Mass.: Allyn and Bacon. cited in Holdren.

Kemmer, Suzanne. June 2000, Week 3. Summary: Earliest Lexical Blending. LINGUIST List 11.1378. Tue. June 20--<http://www.linguistlist.org/issues/11/11-1378.html>

Kimball, Cornell. No Date.--<http://www.barnsdle.demon.co.uk/spell/mini. html>

_____. "Is 'meaning' the answer to bad spelling?" No Date.(Review.) --<http://.www.barnsdle.demon.co.uk.spell/spellrp.html>

Kister, Ken. 2000. "Finally a Cure for Bad Spelling." Stone Cloud Phonics--<http://www.phonicspeller.com/Pages/article-on spelling. html>

Laurita, Raymond E. No Date. The Spelling Doctor's Credo.--<http://www.spellingdoctor.com/Credo.htm>

Levis, John M. 1999. " Training Teachers to Use Written English as a Pronunciation Resource. SPEAK OUT! 24: 16-24. <http//www. public.iasstate.edu/jlevis/ENGL_525/SPEAKOUT_spelling. html>

Magnus, Margaret. 2000. Bibliography of Phonosemantics.--<http://www.conknet.com/~mmagnus/Bibliography.html>

Magnus, Margaret. Linguistic Iconism Association. 2000.--<http:// www.conknet.com/~mmagnus/lia.html>

McCulloch, Myrna. 2000. "Phonics is Phonics is Phonics - or is it?" The Riggs Institute--<http://www.riggsinst.org/artp25.htm>

"Origins of Syriac." Beth Mardutho: The Syriac Institute. 1992-2001.--<http://www.bethmardutho.org/AboutSyriac/>

Orton-Gillingham Phonograms. 2000--<http://www.tutronics.com/overview.htm>

Orton-Spalding Phonograms. 2001--<http://www.riggsinst.org/wordsand.htm>

Post, Reiner. Summary: Folk Etymology. January 1994, Week 1 LINGUIST List 5.20. Tue. Jan. 4.--<http://www.linguistlist.org/ issues/5/5-20.html>

Sebba, Mark. Summary: Social Aspects of Orthography. April 1995, Week1. LINGUIST List 6.489. Mon. 3--<http://linguistlist.org/issues/6/6-489. html>

Sensenbaugh, Roger. 2000 "Phonemic Awareness: An Important Early Step in Learning to Read" ERIC Clearinghouse on Reading, English, and Comunication Digest #119--<http://www.encfacility.net/ericdigests/ed4000530.htm>

Sequoya Cherokee Syllabary. 1999-2000--<http://www.powersource.com/cocinc/language /syllab.htm>

Serbo-Croatian Profile. UCLA Language Materials Project. 2000.--<http://www.lmp.ucla.edu/profiles/profs01.htm>

Simplified Spelling Society--<http://www.spellingsociety.org/about/aims/html>

Suryoyo Online. 1996-2002--<http://www.suryoyo-online.org/>

Upward, Christopher. 2001. "z Less Ambiguous than s" in "Choosing between American and British Spellings as standards for Written English." Simplified Spelling Society.--<http://www.spellingsociety.org/journals/j21/usukspell1.html>

INDEX

BIOGRAPHY

Melvin J. Hoffman is a Professor of English at Buffalo State University College. He teaches Composition, Biblical and Classical Literature, and Linguistics. His website is <http://faculty.buffalostate.edu/hoffmamj/>

He has a Bachelors Degree in English and a Masters Degree in Linguistics from the Illinois Institute of Technology in Chicago. Additionally, he has a Ph.D. in Linguistics from the State University of New York at Buffalo and a Masters Degree in Religious Studies from Canisius College in Buffalo

He has worked as a field interviewer in the dialect atlas survey of Chicago and as a Linguistics Consultant to the Chicago Board of Education. He has also taught inservice classes for the Teacher Corps-Peace Corps, for the Buffalo Board of Education, and for the federal government.

He has published articles in a number of areas. However, the majority of his publications concern African-American Vernacular English, Composition, and Phonosymbolism, respectively.